Year 'Round Dramatic Play

Ages 3-6

by
Gretchen Ballema

D1070375

Published by Totline® Publications
an imprint of
Frank Schaffer Publications®

Author: Gretchen Ballema
Editor: Angella M. Phebus
Interior Designer: Jannette M. Bole

Frank Schaffer Publications®

Totline Publications is an imprint of Frank Schaffer Publications.

Send all inquiries to:
Frank Schaffer Publications
3195 Wilson Drive NW
Grand Rapids, Michigan 49544

Year 'Round Dramatic Play—Ages 3-6

ISBN: 1-57029-533-6

1 2 3 4 5 6 7 8 9 10 PAT 10 09 08 07 06 05

Table of Contents

Introduction

Play is an essential part of a child's development. It is how they learn about themselves and their world. Their actions, curiosity, and imagination create a formula for play. As teachers, we can enhance children's natural inclinations by creating an environment that enriches and promotes play experiences. Dramatic play provides a context for children to channel their playful nature while learning.

Young children are adept at taking common objects and using them to represent other things. Pots and pans become drums, and boxes turn into vehicles or houses. This level of representational play is the beginning of abstract thinking. With the ability to use an object to represent something else, children gain flexibility in their thinking. This type of symbolic play sets the foundation for that flexibility. Soon they will learn to use letters to represent sounds and numerals to represent quantity. Teacher-supported dramatic play offers children the opportunity to learn new things and new concepts. They expand their world and their scientific-knowledge base when they learn about such things as weather and the seasons. Their understanding of social studies grows as they experience the uniqueness of different cultures through supported dramatic play. All of these experiences will be the prior knowledge that is critical for learners when they encounter more complex learning opportunities.

One of the greatest benefits for young children through enriched dramatic play is the opportunity to grow socially and emotionally. Young children naturally move through developmental stages of play. Play which begins from an egocentric point of view grows toward more cooperative actions, from solitary play to parallel play to cooperative play. It is in the highest level of play, cooperative or mature play, that children hone their social and emotional skills. Through interactions with others, children learn much about leadership, negotiating skills, and how to share and take turns. They begin to understand relationships and how their actions impact others.

When young children take on the roles of others, adopting different points of view, they broaden their emotional understandings as well. They learn that others have feelings just as they do. Dramatic play gives children a stage to practice their coping skills as they are asked to share or wait their turn. There are many opportunities to practice problem-solving skills. They must rely on their growing abilities to think of alternatives to problems in their play. What will they do when there is no more food in the play kitchen cupboard? Conflicts may arise as children define their roles in dramatic play. What happens when they all want to be the mommy? These scenarios are golden opportunities for children to think about alternatives, take a turn, or learn to cope with disappointment.

Dramatic play is all about learning through social interaction. Children need to communicate with one another by charting the direction of the play and through the dialogue during the play time. All of these experiences provide ample opportunities to develop their language skills, both oral language and listening skills. Through the many conversations that give life to the drama, children hear new vocabulary used in context and reinforce their growing understanding of the structure, or syntax, of our language. They will practice new words and play with words and the sounds within those words through dramatic play. All of these experiences are fundamental to the development of more sophisticated and complex literacy skills.

Teachers have a critical role in dramatic play. Their role is not that of a playmate, but rather that of a guide. The play is all about the children, and they can do that skillfully. However, to enrich that play, to give it depth and breadth, the teacher has to know when and how to enter the play and when to leave it. Skillful teachers seize those teachable moments, asking questions to move the play to higher levels of thinking. They will weave in and out of the play to give it meaningful direction and to promote learning through their dialogue and thought-provoking questions.

Carefully crafted dramatic play experiences are not just an add-on for fun, they are enriched learning experiences, essential to the healthy social, emotional, physical, and intellectual development of young children.

How to Use This Book

The following pages contain a detailed description of each section of the book. Refer to pages 5–8 frequently as a tool while progressing through each dramatic play idea.

Props and Supplies

The props and supplies for each section are limited only by the imagination! As you collect items for children to use in their dramatic play, think globally and ask, how can this prop be used in other ways? Purchase clear and sturdy plastic tubs for storing dramatic play items. Rotate common play items, and they will seem new again when reemerging. Keep supplies clean and well maintained so children have safe play experiences.

Setting the Stage

Setting the stage means more than just a box of props. It begins with planting the seeds of ideas and possibilities. Lay the groundwork for dramatic play by having many conversations with your children. The time invested in conversations before, during, and after the play will enrich the playful possibilities as one idea often leads to another. Involve the children whenever possible in getting ready for dramatic play. After all, the play is for and all about them!

Through conversations with children, you will also come to understand the extent of their prior knowledge. Support their learning by filling in the gaps with direct conversation, reading-related books, going on field trips, or handling objects relevant to the subject matter. Use correct terms which are appropriate to their developmental level, never talking down to children or using baby talk. Young children delight in the notion that they know and can use big words just like grown-ups.

As you dialogue with children, keep track of their ideas and suggestions by writing them down on chart paper or taking anecdotal notes. Statements made by children will often help "set the stage" for the direction of the dramatic play. It may just move in a different direction! Make clear to children the appropriate use of materials and equipment in each drama. Everything has a place and should be returned to that place when playtime is over. Be sure children take an active role in taking care of their materials. Also, make clear your expectations for their behavior before beginning any of the dramas in this book. In the guided dramas, children need to know what their role is, where they are to go, and what it looks like and sounds like to be an active participant. Tie these expectations into your class rules.

Teacher Talk

Questions and prompts are provided in each section of this book. They are meant as a way for teachers to tickle the imagination of young children, to help move the play into new levels of thinking and into new directions without becoming directly involved in the play. Allow children to respond in their own way and time to the direction that the play takes. You may have one idea, but they may have another. Find ways to call attention to what they are doing during dramatic play. Offer your thoughts sparingly, but productively. Notice a job well done, an effort extended, a problem solved, and give them credit for being so resourceful!

You are a "guide at the side" in dramatic play, not one of the playmates. Teachers who become involved in the play will need to find a graceful way to fade out, allowing the children to do the interacting with one another. Occasionally the teacher will want to become part of the play, but only temporarily and as a means to include other children or give the play a more productive structure.

How to Use This Book (cont.)

Literacy Connections

This section offers a variety of avenues for the teacher to enhance the pre-reading and pre-writing skills in young children. Write the words to songs, fingerplays, and poems on chart paper and/or sentence strips. Make them available to young children so they can explore the written word in connection with the spoken words they're using with each unit. Laminate them for long term use.

Vocabulary Builders

The Vocabulary Builders section includes two parts. The first, *New Words and Word Study,* focuses on specific words or terms used with each unit. The purpose of this is to help children understand the meanings of these words, so they may begin to use them correctly in context. By expanding children's spoken vocabulary they are more likely to have greater success in their reading and writing later on. Preschool- and kindergarten-age children will usually speak in sentence structures using up to eight words. Their vocabulary is somewhere between one and two thousand words. By calling attention to new words and terms, a teacher can have a positive effect on vocabulary development.

The second section is *Onset/Rime.* Understanding how onset and rime work is an essential part of literacy development. It is a facet of phonemic awareness: the ability to hear, isolate, and manipulate sounds. The onset is the beginning part of a word, such as the /c/ in the word *cat*. Rime is the constant ending, the /at/ in *cat*. Each unit has a list of onset and rime words. Many of the words tie directly with the theme or a prominent item in the drama.

Print the words onto tagboard and put together on a word ring or place on a word wall. The purpose of this is twofold. The children will hear the playful nature of words with the same rime, as well as begin to see the spelling patterns in these words. Proficient spellers are able to detect these patterns quickly. Poor spellers have difficulty in doing so and the exposure will help strengthen spelling skills.

Have reasonable expectations for the beginning skill of onset and rime. Do not require that children learn these words. You will have some children who are ready for this type of more formal word activity and some who are not. Know the difference and expect that children will show an interest if they are ready. You are providing exposure to these skills, not an expectation that they master these words.

Write All About It!

Have children create a class library of books. For each dramatic play scenario, direct children in making their own books. Predictable, one-line text will match their pre-reading skills as they work their way through familiar scenes, ones they have acted out in their dramatic play. Provide a special place for these books in the classroom where children can access them easily and often. Consider lending these books to children to take home to read to their families. By the end of the year you will have a large collection of class books. You may choose to disassemble them and return each page to the author/artist, send individual books home with every child to keep, or keep them in the classroom as examples for the next class.

How to Use This Book (The End)

Book Lists

Book lists are provided with each unit, and contain picture books, story books for reading to eager listeners, and/or suitable books for emergent readers to read themselves with a little adult support. Listening to stories read aloud supports young children in learning new words and the structure of language. Select books with delicious words that can be savored and read again. Limited or simple text may work for beginning decoders, but listening to stories with rich language enhances the opportunities for vocabulary development.

Make sure that books become part of the dramatic play area. Content-specific books will serve as a point of reference for growing minds. Fill a basket or a bookshelf with books which are always accessible to the children in the dramatic play area. Vary the titles so there is something fresh and new to read about!

Dramatic Creations

This section allows children to try out their acting skills through guided scripts. Many of the dramas call for children to speak simple and repetitive scripted lines. Write their scripts on sentence strips or cue cards. Support the lines with pictures if necessary. The repetitive nature of the scripts make them easy to learn and fun to recite. Not every child will feel comfortable in taking a role. So honor personal feelings. Often, however, the dramas will have every child involved in some capacity.

Some dramas in this book call for children to listen and follow directions, further enhancing necessary listening skills. Each of these will have the children moving about, acting out a motion, speaking as a group, or some other whole-group activity.

Wrapping It Up

Conclude each drama by engaging in a class conversation. Ask, *what did you enjoy the most about this dramatic play? What changes would you make? What was difficult or challenging for you? Was there anything that didn't work?* Write their comments on chart paper. Make adjustments accordingly for future dramatic play events.

More Seasonal Fun

At the end of each seasonal section you will find additional activities and suggestions to enhance learning. Ideas for art, seasonal book lists, and flannel board activities are listed. Make flannel board pieces out of felt and store them in large manila envelopes. Finger puppet patterns made from felt will allow children another medium to act out the rhymes and word patterns of the fingerplays. When making people for the flannel board, make sure that they represent a variety of ethnic groups.

CD

The CD icon indicates there are added features on the CD such as graphics and songs. When you see this icon, go to the CD to find more resources.

CD

What Did You Do in School Today?

Use the following to help strengthen the home/school connection as well as children's memory skills and perception of time.

Keep anecdotal records of daily class life by writing down memorable events. Gather the class together at the end of each day and reflect on the things they remember. Come to an agreement about one or two things that stand out for the whole group. Bind into a book, or cut out and display ideas in a timeline on a wall. Use language and drawings that are appropriate for your children's understandings. Encourage children to talk about their observations at home.

- Provide a visual reminder of significant events by suspending a hula-hoop from the ceiling. Devote one quarter of the hula hoop space to each season. Draw an eventful experience each week and suspend that cut-out on the hula hoop by tying a string to both the paper drawing and the hoop. Keep the drawing sequential as you tie them onto the hoop, giving children the foundational understanding of the progression of time through the seasons.

- Communicate your seasonal events to parents, so they can continue the conversation and play at home. Provide information in a printed newsletter, orally recap the day when parents arrive to pick up their children, or write brief statements about the play of the day on a white board in a common parent area.

- Another way for children to remember the events which take place at school is to document the action on film. With the advent of digital cameras, photo prints are a click away. Put the printed photos into a photo album and provide simple dialogue to give life to the snap shots. Photo albums will find a place in the classroom library where children can revisit their experiences throughout the year.

- Create a theme-specific poster for each unit by putting photos and children's dialogue onto poster board. When taking photos be sure to have a notepad and pencil handy to write down the children's comments. Provide the dialogue on the posters for the children and their families to read.

- A scrapbook is another way to document each season. Place in it photos and dialogue as described above, along with the children reflections on each season, graphs used during each season (weather, favorites, and so on), and other artifacts which will stir the memories of your children, such as pressed flowers and cut snowflakes.

Props and Supplies

flippers, face masks, snorkels, "air tanks" made from 2L plastic soda bottles, elastic straps, "underwater cameras" made from small boxes, classroom tables, butcher paper, tempera paint and brushes, plastic wrap for portholes, dowels or rulers, sea-life patterns on CD, masking or duct tape, sailor caps made from newspaper, neck scarves, shells, and scooter boards

Setting the Stage

Take a trip under the sea by turning classroom tables into a submarine! Use rectangular classroom tables as the framework for your underwater sub by positioning them end to end. Make sure there is plenty of floor space nearby so the underwater sailors can extend their play by taking a deep-sea dive.

Measure a length of butcher paper equal to the perimeter of the vessel. Have children paint the paper. Subs tend to be grey, but let them use their imaginations and creativity to make the sub their color choice. Cut out portholes for sailors to view underwater life. Use plastic wrap to put over the porthole openings. Tape the butcher paper onto the edge of the tables to create the walls of the sub.

If you do not have butcher paper to use for this project, use blankets or beach towels instead. Use duct tape to secure the fabric to the edges of the tables, so it drapes down and reaches the floor. Create portholes by using clothespins to gather the fabric where windows are desired. Use safety pins above and below the porthole shapes to keep the blanket or towel together, creating the illusion of a window.

Make sure to leave entry and exit doors at opposing ends of the sub. Inside the sub, use a small blanket or towel to section off a portion of the interior to use as an air chamber for transitioning from the inside of the sub to the waters of the deep. One of the main entry/exit doors will be part of the air chamber so the deep-sea divers are able to move through this small section of the sub out into the ocean for some underwater diving fun.

Have children add sea life by creating paper jelly fish, octopi, fish of varying sizes and shapes, and underwater plants. Bring out the water colors to add some color to the underwater creatures. Sea life can be suspended from the ceiling of the classroom by using fish line and heavy-duty tape. Another option is to tie some string to the sea creatures and then tie the other end of the string onto dowels or rulers, which can then be taped onto the top of the table.

As the sailors enter the sub, have them wear paper sailor hats made from folded newspaper. A pre-tied neck scarf can slip over their heads easily, completing their sailor suit.

Once the submarine has found the ocean's floor, it's time to take a deep-sea dive. Children will move to the air chamber where they strap on face masks, flippers, and air tanks made from 2L plastic soda bottles. Tape the soda bottles together using duct tape. The soda-bottle air tanks can be strapped onto the children's backs by using lengths of elastic bands, cut and tied to appropriate lengths, much like a belt.

After the divers have dressed, they may go out and explore the ocean floor. Provide scooter boards so they can swim like the fish as they hunt for treasures, take pictures of sea life, or gather shells from the bottom of the deep sea.

- What do you think you'll find on the ocean floor?
- Do you think you'll find treasure?
- I wonder if you'll discover any new sea life.
- What would you do if you swam up next to a whale?
  (or a shark, sea turtle, sting ray, mermaid...)

Literacy Connections

Songs and Fingerplays

Diving
(Sing to the tune "I'm Bringing Home a Baby Bumble Bee.")

I'm diving in the ocean waters deep.
I've got my fins and flippers on my feet.
I'll swim with fish a while and then I'll float,
Right back to that long grey boat.
(Substitute the color or colors of the submarine they've painted.)

In the Ocean Swimming
(Sing to the tune "The Ants Go Marching.")

I saw a shark a-swimming in the great big ocean
  blue.
I saw a shark a-swimming with another friend or
  two.
I saw a shark a-swimming near,
I said "Hey, let's get out of here!"
And we all swam up to the top of the sea, and
  then, we were free, splash, splash, splash!

Other verses:
I saw a whale a-swimming in the great big ocean
  blue,
I saw an eel a-swimming in the great big ocean
  blue,
I saw a jellyfish swimming in the great big ocean
  blue,
I saw a stingray swimming in the great big ocean
  blue,
I saw a dolphin swimming in the great big ocean
  blue,

There Were 10 Little Fish
(Based on the tune "Ten in the Bed.")

There were ten little fish near the surface of the sea,
And the little one said, "Come and dive with me,"
We're diving, we're diving!

There were nine little fish near the surface of the sea,
And the little one said, "Come and dive with me,"
We're diving, we're diving!

(Continue singing each verse, subtracting one little fish each time until you get to the last little fish.)

Now there's one little fish near the surface of the
  sea,
And the little one said, "I'm as lonely as can be."
So the nine other fish called up to their friend,
And the one little fish went diving in the end.

Vocabulary Builders

New Words and Word Study: Here's a wonderful opportunity to teach children about living creatures that they might not know about! Put up pictures of sea creatures around the classroom and label them. Pictures to consider are: shark, whale, eel, dolphin, stingray, and jellyfish. Use nautical words and terms such as *submarine (sub), air chamber, air tanks, flippers, fins, face mask, snorkel, dive, deep sea, ocean,* and *surface.*

Onset/Rime: Words that have the same spelling pattern as the word *splash*.

/ash/ dash, mash, rash, sash, splash, trash

Write All About It!

Under the Sea Class Book

Have each child create one page for this underwater reading adventure. Ask children to use crayons to draw an underwater "photo," highlighting one item that they might see on a deep-sea dive. Children will also include themselves in the drawing, all suited up in underwater diving gear.

After the crayon drawing is finished, have children use light blue water color to paint over the crayon drawing to add a light wash of "sea water." When the artwork is dry add the text, *When I went diving in the sea, I took a picture of _____ and me."* Ask children to supply the name of the item they saw on their underwater dive.

Book List

- *A Swim through the Sea*, by Kristin Joy Pratt
- *ABC Under the Sea: An Ocean Life Alphabet Book*, by Barbara Knox
- *At the Ocean*, by Gallimard Jeunesse
- *Come to the Ocean's Edge: A Nature Cycle Book*, by Laurence Pringle, Michael Chesworth
- *Exploring the Deep, Dark Sea*, by Gail Gibbons
- *Hidden Under the Sea: The World Beneath the Waves*, by Peter Kent
- *How to Hide an Octopus and Other Sea Creatures*, by Ruth Heller
- *Into the Sea*, by Brenda Z. Guiberson
- *Out of the Ocean*, by Debra Frasier
- *Rub-a-Dub Sub*, by Linda Ashman
- *Seashells by the Seashore*, by Marianne Berkes
- *Small Sea Creatures*, by Jason Cooper
- *Starfish*, by Edith Thacher Hurd
- *Submarine,* by Neil Mallard
- *Under the Sea 1, 2, 3: Counting Ocean Life Book*, by Barbara Knox

 ## Dramatic Creations: The Deep-Sea Dive

This drama calls for fifteen children to participate. For smaller groups of children, make adjustments to the script accordingly. The play begins with the costumed actors (children #1–15) seated in a group. When the narrator gives the signal, all children chant the phrase, "*My friend went diving under the sea and look at what she brought back for me!*" Next, child #1 speaks his or her line and does the corresponding motions. All children chant the familiar phrase again followed by child #1, and then children #2 and #3 speak their line in unison. The chants and responses continue until the five groups of children have spoken their lines. Then the narrator sends the sea creatures back to the ocean.

All children chant: My friend went diving under the sea and look at what she brought back for me!

Child #1: One big blue whale (*Child #1 wearing a blue cape swims in.*)

All children chant: My friend went diving under the sea and look at what she brought back for me!

Child #1: One big blue whale

Children #2 and 3 in unison: Two starfish shining (*Children #2 and 3 wearing gold star headbands walk in with arms and legs extended to resemble the points of a star. Have them walk in without moving their knees!*)

All children chant: My friend went diving under the sea and look at what she brought back for me!

Child #1: One big blue whale

Children #2 and 3 in unison: Two starfish shining

Children #4, 5, and 6 in unison: Three crabs walking (*Children #4, 5, and 6 enter doing the "crab walk." From a seated position, children put their hands on the floor behind them and their legs out in front of them, bent at the knee. Using the muscles in their arms and legs, they lift their torso*

off the floor and walk on their hands and feet.)

All children chant: My friend went diving under the sea and look at what she brought back for me!

Child #1: One big blue whale

Children #2 and 3 in unison: Two starfish shining

Children #4, 5, and 6 in unison: Three crabs walking

Children #7, 8, 9, and 10 in unison: Four lobsters snapping (*Children #7, 8, 9, and 10 wear red mittens and "snap" their "claws" open and shut as they walk in.*)

All children chant: My friend went diving under the sea and look at what she brought back for me!

Child #1: One big blue whale

Children #2 and 3 in unison: Two starfish shining

Children #4, 5, and 6 in unison: Three crabs walking

Children #7, 8, 9, and 10 in unison: Four lobsters snapping

Children #11, 12, 13, 14, and 15 in unison: Five sharks circling (*Children #11, 12, 13, 14, and 15 put their palms together over their heads to resemble the fin of a shark as they move about in a circular pattern.*)

Narrator: There are too many creatures here for me, so all of you fish go back to the sea! (*Children swim away back to a seated position in the circle.*)

Props and Supplies

beach towels and blankets, sun umbrellas, cooler with picnic supplies, clean empty sunscreen bottles, sunglasses, sun hats, flip flops, lawn chairs, hoses and/or water source, seashells, "treasures" (gold spray painted stones), coins, small bags, cardboard surfboards, blue tarp for the water, "sandy" colored fabric for the sandy shore, ocean surf CD, and sand toys: buckets and shovels, beach balls, sand sifters, and small plastic containers such as yogurt or cottage cheese containers for building sand castles

Setting the Stage

Some children are lucky enough to live near the water. Going to the beach may be an everyday occurrence for them. Others may never have the opportunity. Give them a beach experience at the outdoor sand box. Bring child-sized lawn chairs, coolers with play picnic food, picnic tablecloth, beach towels, sunglasses, sun hats, beach umbrellas, and sand toys to the playground "beach."

If your playground does not have a sandbox, consider creating a sand pile by bringing in bags of sand for this experience. To keep the sand clean, cover the sand box or sand pile every evening with a large plastic tarp. This will keep curious neighborhood animals out of the sand.

Fun in the sandbox includes making sand castles and other structures. Provide the children with buckets, shovels, small plastic containers, water to wet the sand, and a hose to rinse off with afterwards. Little paper flags can add decorations to the sand creations. Have children also go on a treasure hunt. Include seashells for finding as well as spray-painted, gold-colored rocks and pennies. Sand sifters of varying sizes will help the discovery process. Provide paper lunch bags to store the finds.

Pretend the surf's up! Give the children props to have surfboarding fun. Using cardboard cut surfboard shapes large enough to accommodate one or two children at a time. Give them crayons to decorate their surfboards. When playtime is over, have the hoses handy for a quick and cool rinse-off before the children re-enter the classroom.

An indoor beach is possible to create as well. Blue plastic tarp or blue vinyl tablecloths create the shoreline. Tan fabric represents the sand. Bring in lawn chairs, picnic supplies, surfboards and shells to complete the scene. A small wading pool can hold sand and toys. Make sure that there is a plastic liner underneath to help with the cleanup. Put on an ocean-surf CD to create the mood of the beach. Provide a whisk broom and dust pan for cleanup.

- How can you sort your shells?
- I wonder if anything interesting will wash up on the shore.
- I wonder what sand is made of.
- How will you stay safe at the beach?
- What different kinds of things can you build with sand?

Literacy Connections

Songs and Fingerplays

Castles on the Shore

(Sing to the tune "Twinkle, Twinkle Little Star.")

Building castles on the shore,
Who could ever ask for more?
Building castles to the sky,
Up to where the birds all fly.
Building castles on the shore,
Who could ever ask for more?

Five Little Seashells

Children will create finger puppets using the pattern provided on the accompanying **CD**.

One little seashell was feeling rather blue,
Along came another and then there were two.
Two little seashells enjoying the breeze,
Along came another and then there were three.
Three little seashells heard the ocean roar,
Along came another and then there were four.
Four little seashells went to take a dive,
Along came another and then there were five.
Five little seashells swimming in the deep,
Feeling rather tired, they all went to sleep.

Sand

Sand on my fingers *(wiggle fingers)*
Sand on my toes *(wiggle toes)*
Sand on my elbows *(point to elbows)*
Sand on my nose *(point to nose)*

Sand on my belly *(rub your belly)*
Sand on my back *(pat back)*
Sand on my ankles *(wiggle feet and point to ankles)*
Sand on my lap *(pat hands on lap)*

A day at the beach is full of sand!
Sand all around and I think it's just grand.
I'll play and I'll build and I'll jump all about! *(play: skip in place; build: pretend to build a sand castle with your hands; jump: jump in place)*
I hope that I can get all this sand shaken out!
(shake your body!)

Vocabulary Builders

New Words and Word Study: Focus vocabulary development on beach-related terms such as *sand, beach, surf, waves, grain (of sand), shore, shells, surfboard, tides, tide pools,* and *seashore.* Some children may not know that ocean water is salty, unlike pool or inland lake water. Explore this idea with them.

Onset/Rime: Words that have the same spelling patterns as the words *fun* and *sun.* /un/ *bun, fun, run, sun, shun, spun*

Write All About It!

One Day at the Beach Class Book

Make several small cumulative books. Limit each book to five or six pages so that text reading for children is manageable. Begin by brainstorming all of the items that might be fun to take to the beach. Write them on chart paper. Have the text for each page reflect the previous pages in the book plus one addition.

Begin with a cover that reads, *One day we all went to the beach and...* The next page is the first child's contribution. As an example, it might read, *Devin took a surfboard, to have some fun.* Subsequent pages will build on this first contribution. Page two could read, *Elise took a bucket, and Devin took a surfboard to have some fun.* Page three builds on the previous text and might read, *Sean took a shovel, Elise took a bucket,* and *Devin took a surfboard to have some fun.* Add a new child's name and item to each page that follows. Ask children to illustrate each page to match the newly added item.

Book List

- *Curious George Goes to the Beach*, by Margret Rey, H. A. Rey
- *At the Beach*, by Anne Rockwell, Harlow Rockwell
- *Biscuit's Day at the Beach*, by Alyssa Satin Capucilli
- *All You Need for a Beach*, by Alice Schertle, Barbara Lavallee
- *Just Grandma and Me*, by Mercer Mayer
- *Tar Beach*, by Faith Ringgold
- *A Day at Seagull Beach*, by Karen Wallace
- *Arthur's Family Vacation*, by Marc Brown
- *On the Beach*, by Alistair Smith, Laura Howell, Ian Jackson
- *Super Sand Castle Saturday*, by Stuart J. Murphy
- *Sisters Are for Making Sand Castles*, by Harriet Ziefert
- *Hattie and the Wild Waves: A Story from Brooklyn*, by Barbara Cooney
- *The Seashore Book*, by Charlotte Zolotow

Under the Sun...A Day at the Beach (The End)

Dramatic Creations: Under the Sun . . . A Day at the Beach

In this drama the narrator uses the hours of the day to sequence a day at the beach. A large, instructional analog clock serves as an additional prop. As each new hour is called out, have a child move the minute hand around the clock once so it is pointing to the corresponding hour. Have the children draw cue cards to illustrate the upcoming actions. As the cue-card directions are being read, children act out each action. With text and pictures on the cue cards, children can take turns being the narrator. Have the narrator read the information on each cue card, giving directions to the young actors.

This play begins with all of the children "sleeping" on the floor. The narrator(s) begins reading from the direction cue cards.

- At 8:00 in the morning, all of the children woke up. They got out of bed, ate their breakfast, and brushed their teeth.

- At 9:00 in the morning, all of the children got ready for the beach. They gathered towels, swimsuits, books, sunhats, sunglasses, buckets, shovels, a picnic lunch, lemonade, and a big beach umbrella.

- At 10:00 in the morning, all of the children hopped in the car to drive to the beach. They turned to the left and they turned to the right. They bounced in their seats until they got to the beach.

- At 11:00 in the morning, all of the children arrived at the beach. They spread out their towels, put on their swimsuits, put on some sunscreen, got out their buckets and shovels, and then stuck their big beach umbrella in the sand.

- At 12:00 noon, all of the children spread out their blankets and ate their picnic lunches.

- At 1:00 in the afternoon, all of the children took a nap.

- At 2:00 in the afternoon, all of the children went for a swim. They put on their life jackets, held their noses, and then jumped in the water! They splashed in the water. They floated in the water. They dove in the water.

- At 3:00 in the afternoon, all of the children dried off with their big fluffy towels. They spread their towels out on the sand, put on their sunglasses and hats, and began to read books.

- At 4:00 in the afternoon, all of the children began to dig in the sand. They shoveled so much sand that it was piled very high. They used their hands to make castles in the sand.

- At 5:00 in the afternoon, all of the children gathered up their things and loaded up the car. They strapped on their seatbelts and rode home.

- At 6:00 in the evening, all of the children were hungry for dinner. They ate and ate and ate and ate until they were very full.

- At 7:00 in the evening, all of the children went for a walk. The looked all around and saw many things. They saw birds in the sky, they saw flowers growing in the gardens, they saw dogs and cats playing, and they saw an ice cream shop. They each had an ice-cream cone. They needed plenty of napkins for all of the drips.

- At 8:00 in the evening, all of the children got ready for bed. They took a bath, they put on their pajamas, they brushed their teeth, they washed their hands and faces, and they brushed their hair.

- At 9:00 in the evening, all of the children went to bed. They turned out the lights, crawled into bed, and pulled up the covers. They closed their eyes and were soon fast asleep.

The Fishing Hole

Props and Supplies

blue tarps or blue vinyl tablecloths, tagboard fish, dowels for fishing poles, string, paper clips, magnets, rubber boots, fishing vests, fishing hats, pipe cleaner worms, bait boxes, fish buckets, blanket or towel to represent the dock, clean empty sunscreen bottles, large cardboard boxes for boats, rope to tie to dock, inflatable raft/boats, life jackets, and fishing nets

Setting the Stage

Get out the poles and put on the rubber boots, it's time to go fishing! Using simple materials, have children create a pond setting for a pretend fishing trip. Whether outdoors under a shady tree, or inside the classroom, the fun will begin with the unrolling of the blue pond tarp.

To set up indoors, begin with a large open area. Move furniture to accommodate the pond. Outdoors, find a level area. Purchase one or more blue plastic tarps or blue vinyl tablecloths to represent the water. Lay them out in the desired configuration. Make sure that the tarps are out of any traffic patterns so the anglers' play is not disturbed.

To create the props needed for this activity, begin with the fish! Using the patterns on the 🅒🅓, print the fish patterns out onto tagboard. Make sure there is a variety available. Have children use different mediums like tempera paint, construction paper, or ribbon, to add features such as scales, eyes, a mouth, and color to bring their fish to life. While decorating the fish, draw attention to both sides of the fish. The colors and patterns drawn on one side should match those on the other side. Do this to strengthen and develop memory skills. When the fish are finished, laminate them for long-term use. Attach a large paper clip near the mouth of the fish.

Make fishing poles with 1/2" dowel and some string. Attach a light-weight magnet to the end of the string for the "hook." For added fun, bait the hook with pipe cleaner worms. Other props to have handy: bait box for the worms, bucket for the caught fish, rubber boots, fishing vests, and caps to wear.

Children can fish from the shore, or add a dock by spreading out a dark-colored beach towel or blanket from the shore into the pond. Or, outline a dock area using wooden unit blocks. Tie up a boat made from a cardboard box, or provide a small inflatable boat for the children to use. Take the boat out into the water, but don't forget the life jackets!

The Fishing Hole (cont.)

- I wonder how many fish you'll catch today.
- What will you do with the fish that you catch?
- How will you sort the fish that you catch?
- Do you think that the fish you catch will stay in the boat?

Literacy Connections

Songs and Fingerplays

Ten Little Fish

Have children use their ten fingers to represent the fish in this fingerplay. You can also ask children to make ten fish out of spring action clothes pins decorating each one as a different fish. Then clip onto the side of a small box or pocket chart. Print words on sentence strips so children can read the lines as they chant. Children may also make fish headbands and act out this fingerplay.

Ten little fish were swimming one day,
Out in the waves and over in the bay.
The first one said, "It's a very hot day."
The second one said. "I'd like to splash and play."
The third one said, "Let's swim where it is cool."
The fourth one said, "Swim over to this pool."
The fifth one said, "I'm as hungry as can be."
The sixth one said, "I see a worm for me."
The seventh one said, "We'd better take a look."
The eighth one said, "Yes, it's on a hook."
The ninth one said, "Let's all swim anyway!"
The tenth one said, "I want to stay."

The last little fish, so very bold and brave,
grabbed a bite of that worm and they all swam away.

At the Clear Blue Water's Edge

(Sing to the tune "London Bridge.")

At the clear blue water's edge
Water's edge, water's edge,
At the clear blue water's edge,
I see a little minnow.

Little minnow swim on by,
Swim on by, swim on by.
Little minnow swim on by,
I see a bright green bullfrog.

Bright green bullfrog hop hop hop,
Hop hop hop, hop hop hop.
Bright green bullfrog hop hop hop,
I see a great big blue fish.

Great big blue fish swish your tail,
Swish your tail, swish your tail.
Great big blue fish swish your tail,
I see a fishing hook!

Have you ever gone fishing?

(Sing to the tune "Have you ever seen a Lassie/Laddie?")

Have you ever gone fishing, gone fishing, gone fishing?
Have you ever gone fishing on a hot summer's day,
With a pole and a hook and a boat and a book?
Have you ever gone fishing on a hot summer's day?

1-57029-533-6 *Year 'Round Dramatic Play*

Vocabulary Builders

New Words and Word Study: Here's a wonderful opportunity to teach children more about a fishing experience! Introduce children to the word *angler* as a non-gender specific term for someone who goes fishing. Other words to use are *bait, fishing rod* and *reel, pond,* and names for some common fish in your region.

Onset/Rime: Words that have the same spelling pattern as the word *fin*.

/in/ *bin, fin, pin, tin, shin, grin, chin, win*

Write All About It!

A Fish Story Class Book

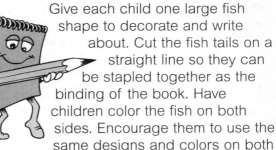

Give each child one large fish shape to decorate and write about. Cut the fish tails on a straight line so they can be stapled together as the binding of the book. Have children color the fish on both sides. Encourage them to use the same designs and colors on both sides of the fish, as is seen in real life. Have children dictate or write a short description about their fish. When the fish is dry, add the writing by putting the text onto a strip of paper and then gluing it to the fish. Use this pattern for this text, *(Child's name)* caught a *(descriptive words such as striped, blue, fat, or scaly)* fish.

BOOK List

- *Fish Is Fish,* by Leo Lionni
- *Ten Little Fish,* by Audrey Wood
- *One Fish, Two Fish, Red Fish, Blue Fish,* by Dr. Seuss
- *Rainbow Fish,* by Marcus Pfister
- *Fish Eyes: A Book You Can Count On,* by Lois Ehlert
- *How Many Fish?,* by Caron Lee Cohen
- *Cat in the Hat: The Fish's Tale,* by Tish Rabe
- *Mr. Putter & Tabby Feed the Fish,* by Cynthia Rylant
- *A Good Day's Fishing,* by James Prosek
- *Thomas Goes Fishing: A Jigsaw Story Book,* by Robin Davies
- *A Boy, A Dog, A Frog, and a Friend,* by Mercer Mayer
- *Squishy Fishie,* by Sue Kueffner
- *Friendly Fish,* by Wendy McLean
- *Fishing for a Dream: Ocean Lullabies and Night Verses,* by Kate Kiesler
- *Canoe Days,* by Gary Paulsen

The Fishing Hole (The End)

Dramatic Creations: A Fish Story

Have one child go fishing for just the right fish in this drama. The "angler" will need a pretend fishing pole with a string attached to go fishing. The "fish" in this drama will find it fun to use scooter boards as they "swim" near the fishing pole. Before you begin this drama, have a conversation with your children about the things they might bring on a fishing trip. Record their responses on chart paper. Use it in this drama for the supplies needed for a day of fishing.

Narrator: Once there was a young girl/boy who wanted to go fishing. She/He said,

Girl/Boy Angler: I will need to take (*Children list the things that she/he will take on this fishing trip from the brainstormed chart paper such as a pole and some string, a tackle box and bait, a pair of boots, a boat, a life jacket, and so on….*)

Narrator: The girl/boy gathered up all the things she/he needed for the trip and went to the lake. There she/he sat down and began to fish. In no time, a school of fish swam up and began to look at the hook.

Fish #1: A worm! I'm hungry!

Fish #2: Me, too, let's eat!

Fish #3: I think I'll take a bite.

Fish #4: Me, too, what a treat.

Narrator: The girl/boy felt a tug on the line and pulled up a fish (*Fish #1*).

Girl/Boy: This fish is too small. (*Fish #1 swims away.*)

Narrator: Then the girl/boy felt a tug on the line and pulled up a second fish (*Fish #2*).

Girl/Boy Angler: This fish is too large. (*Fish #2 swims away.*)

Narrator: Then the girl/boy felt a tug on the line and pulled up a third fish (*Fish #3*).

Girl/Boy Angler: This fish is too old. (*Fish #3 swims away.*)

Narrator: Then the girl/boy felt a tug on the line and pulled up a fourth fish (*Fish #4*).

Girl/Boy Angler: This fish is too young. (*Fish #4 swims away.*)

Narrator: The girl/boy decided that it was time to go home. She/He packed up all of her/his things and thought that perhaps tomorrow would be a better day for fishing.

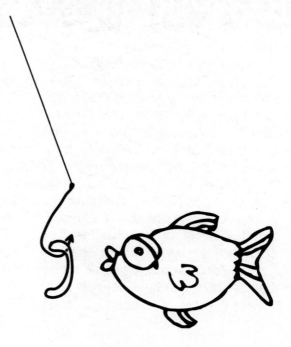

 1-57029-533-6 *Year 'Round Dramatic Play*

Boats Afloat, A Day at the Park

Props and Supplies

child's small molded plastic wading pool, wooden unit blocks, scraps of outdoor carpeting, twigs and paper leaves, artificial greenery, small silk flowers, little plastic people, terry cloth scraps, Tinkertoys®, sanded wood scraps, plastic boats, cardboard paper tubes, wooden craft sticks, glue, small cars, felt strips for roads and sand, play dough, coins, butcher paper, and tempera paint

Setting the Stage

Have children pretend in a model world of their own as they create a miniature park using a small child's swimming pool, scraps of outdoor carpeting, and other building materials. Put a few inches of water in small wading pool, and then add docks and islands using wooden blocks as the foundation. Make sure that the blocks are not completely submerged. The tops should be out of the water. Cut scraps of outdoor carpeting and place them on the islands, covering the blocks.

Guide children in creating the scenery for the park by making trees out of twigs and paper leaves. Play dough makes a good base for "planting" the twig trees. Flowers can be added by using small silk flowers found in craft stores. Use plastic people from any dollhouse set. The little sunbathers can enjoy a day in the sun by using small pieces of terrycloth for beach towels and tan-colored felt for the sand. Make a waterslide for the sunbathers to slide into the water using cardboard paper tubes cut in half lengthwise and supported with wooden craft sticks. Make playground equipment, such as swings, see-saws, monkey-bars, and sandboxes, out of wooden craft sticks and glue.

Use Tinkertoys® or other building materials to build bridges between the islands. Ask children to create roadways for driving small cars on felt strip roads and over bridges. Sail little plastic boats in the bay. Place some coins in the water to represent sunken treasure. Children can make and wear their own sailor caps out of folded newspaper when building and playing with this model water park.

An alternative to bringing water into the classroom is to use a large piece of butcher paper, outlining the water and land on it. Children paint the butcher paper in corresponding colors: blue for the water, green for the land, tan for the sand at the water's edge. Tape the paper onto a sturdy table and begin building the scenery as directed above. Use the same props and let the play begin!

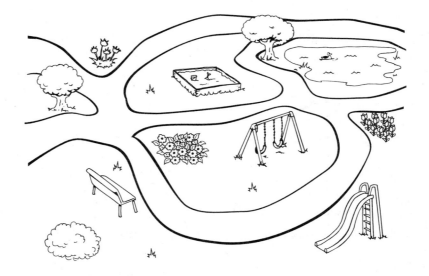

1-57029-533-6 *Year 'Round Dramatic Play*

- I wonder how you could get the little boats to sail across the water without touching them.
- I wonder what would happen if there was a storm.
- Can the boats fit under the bridges? What will you do if they don't?
- How will the swimmers know where it's safe to swim with all of the boats in the water?
- If you don't connect all of the islands with bridges, how else can the people get to them?
- Is there anything else to do at your park? What kinds of things would you like to play with at a park?

Literacy Connections

Songs and Fingerplays

Five Little Boats Went Sailing Out to Sea

Using the template on the (CD), ask children to create finger puppets to wear when chanting this fingerplay.

Five little boats went sailing out to sea.
The first one said, "Sailboats, follow me!"
The second one said, "The waves are getting rough."
The third one said, "The wind is strong and tough."
The fourth one said, "The clouds are getting dark."
The fifth one said, "I think I see a shark!"
The waves swelled high and the winds blew some more,
So they sailed their little boats safely into shore.

In My Pretty Little Park
(Sing to the tune "Twinkle, Twinkle Little Star.")

In my pretty little park,
I could play till way past dark.
Swinging, sliding, swimming, and sun,
Boating, floating, and all kinds of fun.
In my pretty little park,
I could play till way past dark.

I'm Sailing
Write the following on chart paper.

I'm sailing, I'm sailing across the blue sea,
In my little sailboat, just my friends and me.
I'm fishing and swimming, and dodging the waves,
We're fine little sailors who are big and brave.
But in blows a storm and our boats start to rock,
So it's time to go back to our safe little dock.

Vocabulary Builders

New Words and Word Study: Encourage children to use construction vocabulary and words associated with the park that they're building. Words to emphasize are *sink* and *float*, *waves*, *shore*, *beach*, *playground*, *park*, *bridge*, *island*, *highway*, *construct*, and *model*.

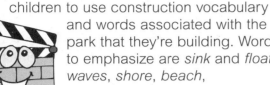

Onset/Rime: Words that have the same spelling pattern as the word *wet*.

/et/ jet, let, met, net, pet, set, fret, wet

Write All About It!

Our Park

Once the model park is complete, ask children to make a map of it. They have a wonderful "bird's-eye" perspective! Allow them to use a clipboard for their paper as they sit by the park to make their map. Have them label things on their map such as beach, bridge, grass, water, and so on. Turn their maps into a class book by providing the repetitive text, *When (child's name) went up in the air, he/she saw _____.* Children dictate/write the completion of the sentence.

Buried Treasure Class Book

Create a class book in the shape of a treasure chest (template on **CD**). Give each child one page to illustrate and write about what they might find in a sunken treasure chest. Use the following sentence. *In (child's name) treasure chest he/she found a(an) _____.*

Book List

- *Row, Row, Row Your Boat*, by Iza Trapani
- *Little Sail Boat*, by Lois Lenski
- *Two Mice in a Boat*, by Katharine Holabird, Helen Craig, Barbara Slade
- *Can You See What I See?: Seymour and the Juice Box Boat*, by Walter Wick
- *Boat Ride with Lillian Two Blossom*, by Patricia Polacco
- *Mr. Gumpy's Outing*, by John Burningham
- *I'm Mighty!*, by Kate McMullan, Jim McMullan
- *The Maggie B.*, by Irene Haas
- *Mr. Putter & Tabby Row the Boat*, by Cynthia Rylant
- *Fireboat: The Heroic Adventures of the John J. Harvey*, by Maira Kalman
- *The Boat Alphabet Book*, by Jerry Pallotta, David Biedrzycki
- *Boat Book*, by Gail Gibbons
- *Me on the Map*, by Joan Sweeney
- *As the Crow Flies: A First Book of Maps*, by Gail Hartman
- *Twins in the Park*, by Ellen Weiss

Dramatic Creations: A Day in the Park

Have children write and direct their own drama by drawing on the elements of their model. Ask children to suggest items they would bring to the park on a warm summer's day. Make a list on chart paper. On a separate sheet of chart paper, list the activities the children suggest they might do at their park.

Give each child two sheets of tagboard. On the first sheet, assign them the task of drawing one thing from the items list. Have the children dictate or write the text to accompany their drawing. The text should read as follows: *For our day in the park, we need (name of item)*. On the second sheet of tagboard, have children illustrate and write an action sentence, which will include how they will use their prop. Punch a hole in the upper left hand corner of each sheet of tagboard in approximately the same place. Once the drawings are created and hole-punched, put them together using a metal book ring for the play, begin with the prop cards and then move to the action cards. Have the prop box handy so the children can gather up the supplies as they are read. Predetermine specific children to gather up the supplies. Ask the narrator to read text such as: *For our day at the park, we need a picnic basket. (Tina gets the picnic basket.) For our day at the park, we need a blanket. (Mary gets the blanket.) For our day at the park, we need sunscreen. (Steven gets the sun screen.)*

After all of the supplies are gathered, read the action cards next. For example: *At the park, we had a picnic with a picnic basket. (Children pretend to spread out their blankets and have a picnic lunch.) At the park, we played ball. (Children pretend to be playing ball.) At the park, we went swimming on our raft. (Children pretend to go swimming on a blow up raft.)* As each action card is read by the narrator, all of the children participate in the actions.

Leave the tagboard cards for this play in the prop box so children can replay this drama over and over again. Allow them to rearrange the sequence of the cards so that the play takes on a new dimension each time!

Props and Supplies

vinyl aprons, clothes line, spring-action clothes pins, towels, wash cloths, sponges, wash tubs, drying racks for dishes, mild bar soap, mild liquid dishwashing soap, bubble solution and wands, glycerin, pipe cleaners, wire coat hangers, large cardboard box bathtub with packing peanuts, back scrubber brushes, net shower scrubbies, shower caps, robes, nail brushes, bath basket, bath toys, clean and empty shampoo, conditioner, and/or body wash bottles

Setting the Stage

Almost every child loves to play in the water and adding bubbles can make water play even more special! Bubbles in water suggest washing things, including ourselves! The housekeeping corner can become sparkling clean as children take on the chore of washing dishes, play food, tables and chairs, and the plastic babies they tenderly care for during the week.

Provide children with two dishpans of water: one with mild sudsy water for washing and the other with clear water for rinsing. A dish-draining rack with a protective rubber mat underneath can accommodate the washed and rinsed items. Be prepared with plenty of towels for drying the washed items and any spills or splashes that occur. Often, hollow plastic food has a little hole in it so it soaks up water. Help children understand this and tell them to make sure the food items are well drained. The same can apply to baby dolls.

This is a good time to wash the furniture as well! Teach children how to squeeze out water from drippy sponges as they tackle the job of washing shelves and cupboard doors. Also use a clothesline and clothes pins to give children the opportunity to wash baby clothing. Everything will smell wonderfully fresh and clean after a day of housekeeping!

Have children take their own "baths" in the classroom by using a large cardboard box and packing peanuts for the soap bubbles. Have large bath towels or beach towels handy for the bathers. Children can enact this fun experience by having back scrubbers, clean empty bottles of shampoo and conditioner, and body wash. Net shower scrubbies and fingernail brushes can be added to the bath basket, along with shower caps and robes. Rubber duckies in the tub? You bet! Some very young children may be inclined to "dress" for the part and may need to be reminded that this is pretend!

As an extension to this activity, supply children with fun bubble-making supplies on the playground. Provide bubble-making solution and wands. Using liquid dish soap, water, and glycerin from a drug store you can make economical bubble solutions. Encourage children to get creative with pipe cleaners, wire coat hangers, or other materials to make their own wands, twisting them into different shapes. Below is a recipe for homemade bubble solution.

> 2/3 cup dish soap
> 1 gallon water
> 2 to 3 tablespoons of glycerin

Use a dishpan for the solution so several children can use it at the same time.

- How will you arrange the food/dishes in the cupboard now that they are clean?
- Now that baby's had his/her bath, what will he/she do next?
- Do you think that having differently-shaped bubble wands will produce differently-shaped bubbles?
- Does it make a difference how hard/softly you blow on your bubble wand?
- What would happen if you let the wind try to blow the bubbles?

Literacy Connections

Songs and Fingerplays

This Is the Way I Take a Bath

(Sing to the tune "This Is the Way We Wash Our Clothes.")

This is the way I take a bath, take a bath, take a bath,
This is the way I take a bath so early in the morning.

Other verses:
Wash my face
Scrub my neck
Suds my back
Wash my hair
Rinse my hair
Scrub my nails
Wash my ears

I'm Cleaning My House

Put the words to the poem below on sentence strips in a pocket chart. Brainstorm with children different action words they would use to talk about cleaning. Write the words on individual cards and substitute them in the underlined positions indicated below. The poem will change as new words are substituted. For ideas, use words from the *Vocabulary Builders* section.

I'm cleaning my house with all my might.
I'll work from dawn until its night.
I'll _____ and _____
And _____ and _____.
My house will shine so sparkling bright!

Five Little Bubbles

Before children begin this fingerplay, have them blow bubbles in the air. See if they can say this fingerplay before all the bubbles float to the ground and pop! Have children make bubble finger puppets using the pattern on the 🅲🅳 so they can share in the bubble action fun.

Five little bubbles floating up so high.
The first one said, "I'm flying in the sky."
The second one said, "It's hot under the sun."
The third one said, "I'm having lots of fun."
The fourth one said, "It's windy way up here."
The fifth one said, "There's nothing to fear."
The wind settled down and they started to drop,
Right down to the ground where they all began to pop!
POP, POP, POP, POP, POP

(Speak each "pop" loudly and with each pop, remove a bubble finger puppet from hand.)

Vocabulary Builders

New Words and Word Study: Emphasize action words used to describe cleaning the house, washing household items, and bathing such as *suds*, *clean*, *scrub*, *rinse*, *dry*, *shower*, *polish*, *wash*, *dust*, and *floating bubbles*.

Onset/Rime: Words that have the same spelling pattern as the words *rub*, *tub*, and *scrub*.

/ub/ *cub, hub, rub, sub, tub, scrub*

Write All About It!

Let's Clean the House

Brainstorm a list of classroom items that need cleaning. Write the list on chart paper. Have children write their names next to the chore(s) they would like each to do. As they complete each chore, ask the children to cross off their names and move on to another task.

If I Were a Bubble Class Book

Provide each child a large, round piece of construction paper with the sentence, *If I were a bubble, high in the sky, I'd look down on the earth and I would spy_____.*

Have children complete the rest of the sentence and then illustrate the item(s) they would see from a floating bubble's perspective. Glue the bubbles onto light blue construction paper and then bind the pages together to form a class book.

Book List

- *Keeping Clean*, by Sharon Gordon
- *Wash Your Hands!*, by Tony Ross
- *Clean Enough, Vol. 1*, by Kevin Henkes
- *Maisy Takes a Bath*, by Lucy Cousins
- *Twins Take a Bath*, by Ellen Weiss
- *Harry the Dirty Dog*, by Gene Zion
- *Eloise Takes a Bawth*, by Kay Thompson, Mart Crowley
- *Bathtime for Biscuit*, by Alyssa Satin Capucilli
- *Just Me in the Tub*, by Mercer Mayer, Gina Mayer
- *Mrs. Wishy-Washy Makes a Splash!* by Joy Cowley, Elizabeth Fuller
- *Tub People*, by Pamela Conrad

- *To Bathe a Boa*, by C. Imbior Kudrna
- *Splash!*, by Roberta Grobel Intrater
- *Splish! Splosh! Why Do We Wash?* by Janice Lobb, Peter Utton
- *Maisy Cleans Up*, by Lucy Cousins
- *Amelia Bedelia*, by Peggy Parish
- *Bubbble Bubble*, by Mercer Mayer
- *Benny's Big Bubble: A Picture Reader*, by Jane O'Conner
- *Simon and the Wind*, by Gilles Tibo
- *I Wonder Why Soap Makes Bubbles* by Barbara Taylor

Dramatic Creations: Bubble Dance

Have children dance like bubbles in the air as they become pretend bubbles! To make giant bubble props, cut large circular bubble shapes out of sturdy paper. Provide children with bubble solution tinted with blue tempera paint. Guide them in blowing bubbles onto the paper. Put plenty of newspaper underneath. When dry, use the bubbles as a dance prop for the drama below.

Also needed are some dishes. Have children create dinner dishes. On the back side of the bubble prop ask children to draw some of their favorite foods or cut and paste on food items from magazines.

Have the narrator create a context for the dance by using the guided imagery detailed below in the drama. Ask children to act out each of the narrator's directions. The narrator will allow time between directions for the children to fully participate in each action. Tell children to hold their bubble/dish creations against their chests so only one side can be seen.

Narrator:

- Pretend you are all lying on the bottom of a dish pan. *(Children are holding their paper bubbles as they lay on the floor.)*

- Here comes the water. It feels so warm. *(Narrator pretends to be pouring water on the bubbles.)*

- I'm stirring up the water. *(Narrator moves among the children bubbles.)*

- The bubbles slowly begin to grow! *(Children begin to slowly rise from the floor to a seated position.)*

- The water comes faster now. *(The narrator adds more water.)*

- Here come the dishes! *(Some or all of the children can flip their bubble painting to the dish side of the paper and mingle among the bubbles.)*

- The washcloth is stirring up the water. *(The narrator moves among the bubbles and dishes with a beach towel.)*

- The last dish is finished. *(Children holding the dish side of the paper flip it to the bubble side and all of the dishes are gone.)*

- The plug is pulled and all the water and suds go down the drain! *(Children find a place on the floor and lay down once again.)*

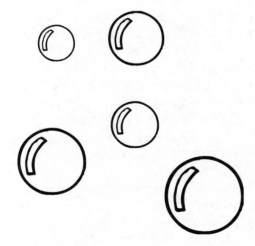

It's Raining, It's Pouring

Props and Supplies

large plastic sheeting or tarps, clothesline, spring-action clothes pins, tent stakes or other weights for securing the bottom of the shelter to the ground (or use a waterproof tent), lawn sprinkler, garden hose, lawn chairs, outdoor carpet, books, drawing materials, blocks, rain coats, rain hats, rubber boots, umbrellas, and bathing suits

Setting the Stage

A summer rain shower can be loads of fun, especially on a hot and sunny day. Use heavy-duty plastic sheeting or plastic tarps to create a shelter where children can stay dry from an impromptu summer shower created by a garden hose and a lawn sprinkler.

To build the lean-to shelter, begin by using a large plastic tarp and a length of sturdy clothesline. Tie the clothesline to stationary items outdoors, such as trees or playground equipment. Drape the tarp over the clothes line so that about one foot of it hangs over the open side of the shelter. Secure the tarp with spring-action clothes pins. Use plenty of clothes pins to keep it in place so the shelter can stand up to the pounding rain shower.

Draw the bottom of the tarp away from the centerline and secure it to the ground using tent stakes, long pieces of wood, or other heavy items. Allow about a foot of extra plastic sheeting on the ground to extend away from the shelter side of the structure. This will allow the water to move away from the lean-to, keeping the ground inside the shelter dry and mud free. Position the sprinkler on a downward slope from the plastic tent sheeting so that the water drains away from the shelter. If you have a water-proof tent, you can use that as a substitute.

Bring some lawn chairs and a piece of outdoor carpeting inside the shelter. Supply the summer shelter with books, drawing supplies, and blocks to have some relaxing fun inside and out of the rain.

For fun outside of the shelter, add rain coats, rubber boots, and umbrellas for a walk in the rain.

Now, turn on the sprinkler so the water spray hits the plastic sheeting. You've created a sunny-rainy day! Keep an eye out for those rainbows!

1-57029-533-6 *Year 'Round Dramatic Play*

- How does the "rain" sound on the "roof" of our lean-to?
- What words would you use to tell how it sounds?
- Can you think of any other words for "rain"?
- How would you feel if you were caught in the rain?
- What do you think the forest animals do in the rain?
- Where do you think the rain goes once it hits the ground?

Literacy Connections

Songs and Fingerplays

Little Raindrops

(Sing to the tune "Are You Sleeping?")

Little raindrops, little raindrops,
Falling down, falling down.
See the little raindrops,
Drippy, drippy raindrops,
Falling down, falling down.

See the lightning, see the lightning,
Flashing bright, flashing bright.
See the flashing lightning,
Lighting up the night time,
Flashing bright, flashing bright.

Hear the thunder, hear the thunder,
Boom, boom, boom!
Boom, boom, boom!
Hear the booming thunder,
Rumbling, tumbling thunder,
Boom, boom, boom,
Boom, boom, boom!

Pretty rainbow, pretty rainbow,
Shining bright, shining bright.
Red, yellow, and orange,
Green, blue, and purple,
Shining bright, shining bright.

I See the Rain a Coming

(Sing to the tune "The Ants Go Marching.")

I see the rain a coming and the wind begins to blow.

I see the rain a coming and the wind begins to blow.
The wind it blows and clouds are grey.
The bright sunshine all went away.
And the rain is coming down, in the town, on the ground.
Rain, rain, rain.

Other verses:
hear
feel
taste
smell

The Colors of the Rainbow

Use this poem to help children recognize color words. Write each line of text on sentence strips, using the correct color for the color words. Use rebus pictures on tagboard to cover words. For example, draw red roses on a card and place over the word roses. As the children learn the poem, the rebus pictures will no longer be necessary.

Red like the roses growing on a vine,
Orange like the sunset and a day that's fine,
Yellow like the daffodils growing on the hill,
Green like the color of a brand new dollar bill,
Blue like the robin's eggs lying in a nest,
But, purple is the color that I like the best!
Colors of the rainbow shining bright,
Colors of the rainbow slipping out of sight.

Vocabulary Builders

New Words and Word Study: Extend children's oral and written vocabulary by using  synonyms for *rain* and *rainy weather*. Cut out a large raindrop and as new words for rain emerge, write them on the paper raindrop. Keep the raindrop word bank on the wall to write down new words. For example, *sprinkles, showers, drizzle, downpour.*

As children discuss the path that a raindrop might take, bring up words like *puddle, stream, brook, river, lake, bay, sea, ocean.* Other words to consider: *rainbow, cloud, droplets,* and new color words, such as *violet.* Ask children to think of other color words, such as *scarlet* for *red.*

Onset/Rime: Words that have the same spelling pattern as the word *drop.*
   /op/ *hop, mop, pop, top, drop, stop*

Write All About It!

If I Were a Raindrop Class Book

Ask children to write or dictate a story and illustrate. Have children use their imaginations while thinking about what happens to raindrops once they reach the ground.

Each page will have the same predictable text, *If I were a raindrop I would _____.* Possible responses are: "help the flowers to grow," "make a mud puddle," "flow into the river." Keep responses limited to the completion of the sentence. By doing so, children are better able to read the text themselves. The limited text will resemble the emergent reading levels they will see in reading lessons.

Book List

- *Rain Feet*, by Angela Johnson
- *Mushroom in the Rain*, by Mirra Ginsburg
- *Rain Romp: Stomping Away a Grouch Day*, by Jane Kurtz
- *What Can I Do When It Rains?*, by Pamela Zagarenski
- *Splosh!*, by Mick Inkpen
- *Red Rubber Boot Day*, by Mary Lyn Ray
- *Cat and Mouse in the Rain*, by Tomek Bogacki
- *Here Comes the Rain*, by Mary Murphy
- *Rain Dance*, by Kathi Appelt
- *Rain, Vol. 1*, by Robert Kalan
- *Jack: It's a Rainy Day*, by Rebecca Elgar
- *Splish, Splash*, by Marcia Leonard
- *Soggy Saturday*, by Phyllis Root
- *Adventures of Drippy, The Runaway Raindrop*, by Sidney Sheldon
- *Wet World*, by Norma Simon

Dramatic Creations: Rain Dance

Use a roll of blue crepe paper streamers and a little tape to transform children into a rain shower! Flowing from arms, waists, shoulders, and as headbands, children dance to the music of Vivaldi's Summer selection of the Four Seasons. Encourage children to listen to the music and imagine how they might dance to this timeless music.

Dramatic Creations: Rainbow in the Sky

Prepare color words on pieces of tagboard, using the corresponding color marker to write the color name. Ask the narrator to hold up the color word card as it is called out.

Narrator: One day there was a terrible storm.

(Children use cymbals for thunder and flashing flash lights for lightning.)

Narrator: The wind was howling.

(Children make a "whooooing" wind noise.)

Narrator: The storm started to pass and the sun peeked out from behind the clouds. When the sun shone through the last rain drops, a rainbow formed. First there was red.

(All the children with the color red on come into the circle and do a little dance, then they return to their seats. As an alternate, have children wear crepe paper streamers of different colors.)

Narrator: Then there was orange.

(Children wearing orange come into the circle to dance.)

Narrator: Yellow followed behind.

(Children wearing yellow come into the circle to dance.)

Narrator: Next came green.

(Children wearing green come into the circle to dance.)

Narrator: Blue took its turn.

(Children wearing blue come into the circle to dance.)

Narrator: Violet finished the rainbow.

(Children wearing violet come into the circle to dance.)

Narrator: Then all the colors of the rainbow could be seen.

(All children dance.)

Narrator: When the rain stopped and the sun ducked back behind a cloud again, the rainbow was gone.

(All children sit down.)

Props and Supplies

plastic buckets with handles, paint brushes of varying sizes, water, painters hats, wooden stirring sticks, vinyl aprons, butcher paper, tempera paints, artists brushes in varying sizes, used clean paint cans (Avoid old paint cans as they may have contained lead-based paint.)

Setting the Stage

Most young children love to paint. They can approach a blank sheet of paper and without hesitation apply colors in varying patterns and shapes. They get pleasure in doing and watching as the colors mix together to form interesting designs and even new colors. Give them the opportunity to take a painting experience outdoors as they pretend to be house painters. For this experience, they'll be using water instead of paint!

Provide children with clean paint cans or plastic buckets and paint brushes of varying sizes, suitable for painting houses. Put a few inches of water in the paint cans and "paint" the outside of the building or surrounding structures such as a deck, patio, wooden play structure, and so on. Visit a local paint shop to pick up painters caps and wooden stirring sticks. Vinyl aprons help protect children's clothing, or have the children wear swimwear.

If the day is hot and sunny, the painters may soon discover their work has disappeared! Evaporation is a difficult concept for young children to comprehend; however, the experience will lay the groundwork for scientific concepts they will learn in the future.

As an alternate experience, suggest to children they can create a mural painting outdoors. If your community has murals, arrange a trip to see them. A mural is not graffiti. It is a work of art that represents a message or tells a story. Give children the opportunity to plan before they begin painting. Decide what story or message they will tell in the mural and make a list of the elements they will be including. A suggested topic for their first mural is a day at school. *What things happen at school? How would you paint those activities?*

To have your children be mural painters, provide long sheets of butcher paper, water-based tempera paint, and brushes of varying sizes. Either affix the paper to the side of the building or on a fence, or lay the paper on the ground. Either way, protect the ground surface by laying down newspaper or plastic sheeting. Let children know that this activity requires special permission from the building owner and they are not to paint directly on the building or fence.

Painting Time (cont.)

- Look at where you painted. It seems dry now. What happened to the water?
- What else can you "paint"?
- What kinds of designs can you make with your "paint"?
- Have you ever seen water "disappear" before?
- What story does your mural tell?
- What do you think happens to the tempera paint? It starts out wet and then it dries. What's going on?

Literacy Connections

Songs and Fingerplays

This Is the Way We Paint the House

This is the way we paint the house, paint the house, paint the house.
This is the way we paint the house, so early in the morning.

Additional verses: This is the way we paint the (deck, fence, patio, porch, post, garage, swings, and so on.)

I'm Painting the House Today

(Sing to the tune "Farmer in the Dell.")

I'm painting the house (deck, fence, garage) today.
I'm painting the house today.
I'll use my brush to leave a blush
Of paint on it today.

Five Little Painters

Use the paintbrush pattern on the 🔘 to create finger puppets for this fingerplay.

Five little paintbrushes, standing all ready.
The first one said, "Keep your hands real steady."
The second one said, "Let's all paint the door."
The third one said, "No, let's all paint the floor!"
The fourth one said, "The wall's the place for me."
The fifth one said, "Please, let's all agree."
So the five little brushes used blue and green and red.
And they painted all the things they saw, cleaned up, and went to bed.

What Color Should I Paint My House?

Write the following on chart paper.

What color should I paint my house?
It needs a coat of paint!

I think I'll paint it red today!
(Hold up a card with the word "red" written on it in red. All children wearing red stand up and begin to "paint," then sit down again in the circle.)
No, red is not the way!

I think I'll paint it orange today!
(Hold up a card with the word "orange" written on it in orange. All children wearing orange stand up and begin to "paint," then sit down again in the circle.)
No, orange is not the way!

(Continue on using additional colors: yellow, green, blue, violet, white, black, brown, tan, etc. Conclude with...)

What color should I paint my house?
I really can't decide.
So I shall paint my little house
All the colors I have tried!
(All children stand and paint!)

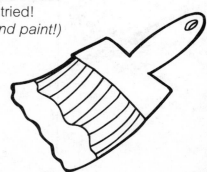

Vocabulary Builders

New Words and Word Study: The concept of evaporation will be beyond the understanding of young children, but they will see the evidence of it as their water-paint disappears! Use the term *evaporation* as you discuss what happens to the water they've just brushed on to the side of the building or cement sidewalk. Other words such as *disappear*, *air*, *atmosphere*, and *clouds* will add to this difficult concept. While the children are painting, use terms such as *brush strokes*, *drips*, *drops*, *evenly*, and *mural*.

Onset/Rime: Words that have the same spelling pattern as the word *red*.

/ed/ bed, fed, led, red, shed, sled

Write All About It!

Let's Paint Class Book

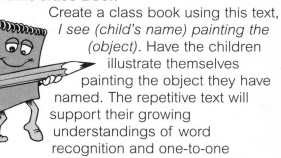

Create a class book using this text, *I see (child's name) painting the (object)*. Have the children illustrate themselves painting the object they have named. The repetitive text will support their growing understandings of word recognition and one-to-one correspondence in reading words.

A Mural's Story

Once the class mural from the dramatic play is dry, have children dictate/write a message which tells the story of their portion of the class painting. Keep the text to a minimum so children are able to "read" it. Add the text by writing it on separate pieces of paper and gluing it near the appropriate part of the painting.

- *George Paints His House,* by Francine Bassede, Dominic Barth
- *Max Paints the House*, by Ken Wilson-Max
- *The Wilsons, a House-Painting Team*, by Alice K. Flanagan, Christine Osinski
- *Big Brown Bear*, by David McPhail
- *Mr. Pine's Purple House*, by Leonard Kessler
- *The Big Orange Splot*, by Daniel Manus Pinkwater
- *Toolbox Trouble: A Busy Bugz Book*, by Christine Tagg
- *Green Bear*, by Alan Rogers

Dramatic Creations: The House Painters

For this drama, create paintbrushes using the pattern on the **CD**. Print them onto tagboard. Write the color name on the handle and then color the bristles with the corresponding color. Place the completed paintbrushes in a clean and dry paint bucket, so the handles can be seen. Select a child to be the house owner. Several children approach the house owner to paint his or her house. The action is lead by the narrator. Be sure to use the appropriate pronouns throughout.

Narrator: Once there was a boy who wanted to have his house painted. He asked *(select a children from the group)* if she would paint his house.

Homeowner: "Will you paint my house?"

Painter #1: "Yes, I will."

Homeowner: "Please paint my house *(color name)*."

Narrator: So the painter found her brush and began painting. *(Painter #1 selects that color brush from the bucket and pretends to paint the house.)*

Narrator: The painter finished the job and left *(child sits down)*. The boy looked all around the house and decided that he didn't like the color. He called another painter to come and paint the house again.

Homeowner: Will you paint my house?

Painter #2: Yes, I will.

Homeowner: "Please paint my house *(color name)*."

Narrator: So the painter found his brush and began painting.

(Painter #2 selects that color brush from the bucket and pretends to paint the house.)

Narrator: The painter finished the job and left *(child sits down)*. The boy looked all around the house and decided that he didn't like the color. He called another painter to come and paint the house again.

(The drama continues in the same pattern until the last color is painted. The drama concludes with the following...)

Narrator: The painter finished the job and left. The boy looked all around the house and decided that the color was just right.

Something Extra!
A Lively Mural

A mural is a painting that tells a story or conveys a message. Once the children have painted a mural on butcher paper, find a place in the classroom to hang it at their level.

Children will either move along the mural painting and act out the various scenes from the mural, or several children will find a position next to the painting and act out that one component of the mural.

The Car Wash

Props and Supplies

Props and Supplies

tricycles and/or big-wheel bikes, sponges, buckets, garden hoses, small mist squirt bottles, cash register, play money, rubber boots, towels, large appliance box, terry cloth fabric strips for "scrubby" arms inside the car wash, chairs and magazines for the waiting room

Setting the Stage

Hook up the garden hoses and get out the bikes; it's time to clean them up at the pretend car wash! Create an outdoor car wash by first chalking an outline of the drive-through car wash on a patch of playground cement or blacktop. The outline will provide the driver with a course to follow from start to finish. If a hard surface such as cement is not available, pick out a grassy spot on the playground, one that won't create a lot of mud when the water starts to flow! Use wooden blocks, small stakes, or little flags to define the path of the car wash.

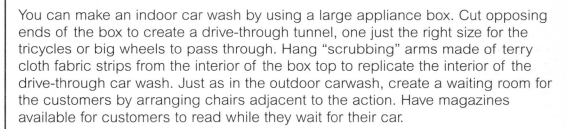

Have the customers drive their tricycles or big wheels up to the entrance. There they read the menu of car wash options and then pay the car wash manager the correct amount of money. Station a comfortable waiting room nearby so customers can relax while their car gets cleaned. While the customer waits, the workers wash the cars using buckets of mild sudsy water and sponges. They drive the tricycles or big wheels through the car wash course to the other end. Workers will then use hand towels for drying the cars. Lastly, the sparkling clean cars are returned to their owners.

You can make an indoor car wash by using a large appliance box. Cut opposing ends of the box to create a drive-through tunnel, one just the right size for the tricycles or big wheels to pass through. Hang "scrubbing" arms made of terry cloth fabric strips from the interior of the box top to replicate the interior of the drive-through car wash. Just as in the outdoor carwash, create a waiting room for the customers by arranging chairs adjacent to the action. Have magazines available for customers to read while they wait for their car.

Have children create signs to advertise the pretend car wash, as well as a menu of options for the customers to select from. Provide the manager of the car wash with a cash register to do business.

With tricycles on the playground or in the classroom, establish traffic rules for children to follow. One-way streets work well. Use stop signs at pedestrian crossings so children know how to safely travel amidst the traffic. Issue driver's licenses to the young drivers. Just like in the real world, they might get a ticket if they don't follow the rules of the road!

Published by Totline Publications. Copyright protected.   1-57029-533-6 *Year 'Round Dramatic Play*

- How are you going to get customers to come to your car wash?
- What are the parts of the tricycles that you're willing to wash: tires, seats, handlebars?
- What will you do if it rains? Do you think people will still pay money to get their car washed? Should you lower the price?
- What if someone wants their wagon washed?

Literacy Connections

Songs and Fingerplays

This Is the Way We Wash the Car

This is the way we wash the car,
   wash the car, wash the car.
This is the way we wash the car so early in the
   morning.

Other verses:
This is the way we wash the wheels.
This is the way we wash the windows.
This is the way we dry the car.
This is the way we vacuum the car.
This is the way we wax the car.

Drive My Car to the Car Wash

(Sing to the tune "Take Me Out To the Ball Game.")

Drive my car to the car wash.
Take it there to get clean.
Wash off the dirt and all the dust.
Wipe it dry and don't let it rust.
Oh I'll drive my car through the car wash.
They'll clean it up till it shines!
For its one, two, three coats of wax at the old
   car wash.

The Car Wash

Today is the day I'll wash my car.
   *(Make circular washing motions with their
   hands.)*
It's been to places both near and far.
   *(Near, put palms close together; Far, stretch
   arms out far apart.)*
It's coated with dirt and dust, that's true.
   *("Dust" off arms by brushing them with opposite
   hand.)*
It's time to make it sparkle like new.
   (Hold up hands and wiggle fingers.)
But look, what's that in the sky I see?
   (Look up with hand shading eyes.)
A big grey cloud hanging over me!
   (Place arms together overhead forming a circle.)
Well, maybe today's not the day.
   (Fold arms and put one hand on chin.)
I think the rain is here to stay!
   *(Lift up arms and slowly lower hands making
   rain motions with fingers.)*

Vocabulary Builders

New Words and Word Study: Most children only know one word for cars, and that's the word *car*! Help them to learn there are other words: auto, *automobile*, and *vehicle*. During the car washing, make a point to emphasize the action words they'll be doing: *spray*, *squirt*, *polish*, *dry*. Use describing words to highlight the terrific cleaning job such as *shining*, *sparkling*, *squeaky clean*, and so on. Other words to use are *pedestrian*, *traffic*, and *cross walk*.

Onset/Rime: Words that have the same spelling pattern as the word *car*.

/ar/ bar, car, far, jar, tar, star

Write All About It!

The Crazy Car Wash Class Book

In this class book, have children write about a crazy car wash. One where a car is driven in, but a different vehicle comes out the other end of the car wash. The first page will read, *We all went to the Crazy Car Wash. We all drove our cars in, but when we drove out....* Subsequent pages follow a predictable pattern and reflect the new vehicle that emerges from the crazy car wash, *(Child's name) was driving (another kind of vehicle, such as a truck, motor home, motor cycle, bike, train, bus, and so on).*

Encourage children to use describing words such as a *shiny truck*, *huge motor home*, *black motorcycle*. Ask children to illustrate the text on their page of the book, matching the illustrations to their descriptions.

Book List

- *Five Little Monkeys Wash the Car*, by Eileen Christelow
- *Wash Me*, by John Youssi
- *Big Yellow Taxi*, by Ken Wilson-Max
- *Cars, Trains, Planes, and Trucks*, by Nancy Rinolone
- *Cars and Trucks and Things that Go*, by Richard Scarry
- *Car Wash*, by Sandra Steen, Susan Steen
- *Car Wash Kid*, by Cathy Goldberg Fishman
- *The Scrubbly-Bubbly Car Wash*, by Irene O'Garden
- *Sluggers' Car Wash*, by Stuart J. Murphy, Barney Saltzberg
- *Dad's Car Wash*, by Harry A. Sutherland, Maxie Chambliss

The Car Wash (The End)

Dramatic Creations: The Car Wash Wave

Have children sit in a circle. The leader begins by demonstrating the first motion. Each child repeats the motion going around the circle until it comes back again to the leader. The leader then does the second motion, which goes around the circle once again. Each motion proceeds in like manner.

- Start your car engine. *(Turn the key with your right hand.)*
- Turn the car to the right. *(Hands on steering wheel and turn the wheel to the right.)*
- Turn the car to the left. *(Hands on steering wheel and make a turn to the left.)*
- Put on the brakes. *(Extend the right foot and push down hard.)*
- The car wash begins with a spray. *(Claps hands together as if holding a garden hose and spray back and forth.)*
- Scrubby "arms" help wash the car. *(Wiggle arms up and down in front of you.)*
- Water squirts on the car. *(Extend arms in front of you with one arm above the other with palms in a vertical position. Move arms together in a back and forth manner, wiggling your fingers to indicate water spraying.)*

- The air blowers dry the water. *(Cup both hands around your mouth and blow.)*
- Wax the car till it shines. *(Put both hands in front of you, palms facing away from your face, and make circular motions with each hand as if rubbing wax on and off.)*
- Drive off again in a clean car! *(Both hands on the wheel, bounce up and down from a seated position on the floor.)*

Will You Wash My Car?

In this activity, children ask a car wash employee if they may have their car washed. When a child approaches the car wash employee they ask, *"Will you wash my car?"* The employee pulls a line of script from a basket and reads the reply.

Suggested replies include: *"No, it's too _____."* The employee fills in the blank with a describing word, such as *wide, thin, short, tall, old, junky,* and so on. Have one card that reads, *I will be happy to!*

When the card is drawn and read, the customer who requested to have his or her car washed then becomes the manager and the play continues. Customers line up and the requests begin again until the *I will be happy to!* card is drawn again, at which point the roles trade again.

 1-57029-533-6 *Year 'Round Dramatic Play*

Summer Art Activities

Summer Trees: Have children create their own summer trees by using a full sheet of light blue construction paper. Ask them to use a brown crayon to draw a large tree, the full height of the paper. Once the trunk and branches are complete, add green summer leaves. Cut various shades of green tissue paper into 1" squares. Children then take individual squares and put them onto the eraser side of an unsharpened pencil, positioning the eraser in the center of the tissue paper square. Bunch up the ends of the tissue paper along the sides of the eraser, creating a cup-like shape. Apply one dot of glue onto the tree where the tissue paper leaf will be placed and then use the pencil to place the tissue paper leaf onto the glue. Fill the tree with lots of leaves!

Class Summer Tree: Cut a 6' or greater length of butcher paper and outline the trunk and branches of a tree. Have children paint the tree trunk and branches with brown paint. Once the paint is dry, children add leaves. Supply green construction paper for the leaves, which the children will tear into leaf shapes. Demonstrate how to tear the paper by making small tears instead of large rips. Apply the leaves with glue. When the tree is dry, hang it in the classroom.

Faded Prints: The sun is a powerful source of energy. Employ it to make these faded prints using vividly-colored construction paper and everyday objects. Have children arrange a collage of interesting shapes onto vividly-colored construction paper. Red, green, royal blue, purple, and dark brown will produce excellent results. Place the collage in direct sunlight, and be careful not to move the objects! After several days, remove the objects and observe the results!

Sand Paintings: Guide children in using construction paper to create sand paintings. Have them apply thin lines of glue directly from plastic glue bottles onto paper. Once the glue has been applied, have children sift clean beach sand onto the glue. Next, have them flip the paper and let the loose sand fall off onto the newspaper-covered table. By applying the glue in thin lines and dots, the glue will not run or drip as easily, which will keep the sand in place.

Sponge Painting: Cut sponges into small sizes and various shapes for sponge painting with tempera paint. Dip damp sponges into the paint, dabbing off the excess paint, and then print with the painted sponge onto construction paper. Some children may not like holding the painted sponges. Use spring-action clothes pins to hold the sponges during the painting process if desired.

Chalk Shadow Drawings: Young children enjoy taking colorful chalk out onto the playground cement and creating their own art work. Give them a different option for this medium by asking them to draw shadows! While one child stands and casts a shadow onto the cement, a second child outlines the shadow. Be sure to draw the outline of the child's feet, too, because they will be come back to this same spot later on. After a short time, perhaps an hour or more, have the pair go back to their shadow and ask the first child to stand where he or she stood the first time, positioning his or her feet in the outline drawn previously. What has happened? Draw a second outline, or perhaps even a third, as the day goes by. Talk about why the shadow outlines are drawn in different places.

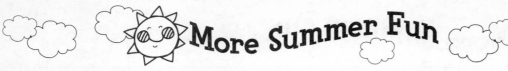 **More Summer Fun**

Book List for Summer

- *Summertime in the Big Woods*, by Laura Ingalls Wilder
- *Hot Dog*, by Molly Coxe
- *Hot City*, by Barbara Joosse
- *One Hot Summer Day*, by Nina Crews
- *It's Summer*, by Jimmy Pickering
- *Letter to the Lake*, by Susan Marie Swanson, Peter Catalanotto
- *Summer's Vacation*, by Lynn Plourde
- *Marshmallow Kisses*, by Linda Crotta Brennan
- *Cool Ali*, by Nancy Poydar
- *It's Summertime!*, by Elaine, W. Good, Susie Shenk Wenger
- *When the Fireflies Come*, by Jonathan London, Terry Widener
- *It's Summer!*, by Linda Glaser, Susan Swan
- *When Summer Comes*, by Robert Maass

Flannel Board

Create felt pieces for children to use on a flannel board while exploring the following dramatic play themes.

Under the Sea…A Swim with the Fish

divers, flippers, fins, air tanks, snorkels, underwater plants, a variety of fish, submarines, shells, and a treasure chest with golden treasure

Provide ten fish for the children to sing along with "There Were 10 Little Fish."

Under the Sun…A Day at the Beach

sun, sunbathers, beach towels, sun umbrellas, seashells, surfboards, buckets, shovels, sandy beach, waves, sand castles, and analogue clocks with hourly times to accompany the drama "Under the Sun…A Day at the Beach"

Provide five seashells for the "Five Little Sea Shells" fingerplay.

The Fishing Hole

blue pond water, fish, fishing poles, worms, anglers, fish buckets, a variety of boats, and docks

Boats Afloat, A Day at the Park

blue pond water, a variety of boats, islands, trees, sandy beach, people, picnic basket, dogs, swings, slide, felt strips for building bridges, and cars

Soap, Bubbles, and Bath Time

bubble wands, bubbles of varying sizes, a bather's head, shampoo bottle, towel, dishes, and dish pan, clothes, and clothesline

Provide five bubbles with faces for the "Five Little Bubbles" fingerplay

It's Raining, It's Pouring

grey clouds, raindrops, rainbows, sun, umbrellas, people, raincoats, boots, rain hats, rain shelters, and puddles

Painting Time

colored paint buckets with corresponding colored paintbrushes all labeled with the color names, and a variety of differently colored houses

The Car Wash

variety of cars and trucks, buckets, car-washing clothes and brushes, a model car wash, and roads

Provide a large car so children may wash it as in the song "This is the Way We Wash the Car."

Down on the Farm

Props and Supplies

red bulletin board paper, construction paper, tempera paints, paintbrushes, shoeboxes, shredded paper "straw," white and brown plastic eggs, bucket for milking the cow, short stool, brown paper grocery bags, brown cardboard boxes, bailing twine, egg basket, empty egg cartons, 3' by 3' piece of 4" to 6" thick upholstery foam, plastic vegetables, small plastic hand trowel, free standing wooden puppet theater, clean milk cartons, cottage cheese containers, yogurt containers, and butter tubs

Setting the Stage

Turn your classroom into Old MacDonald's farm by creating barnyard scenery out of simple materials. Using rolls of red bulletin board paper, cut and tape together the outline of a barn. Have children add details to the barn structure by painting doors, windows, and a roof. Using construction paper, add a weathervane to the top of the barn.

Once the barn is complete, add the animals! Every farm needs a milk cow. Have children paint a cow on butcher paper. Add a milking bucket and a stool for fresh dairy products from the farm. Pour the pretend cow's milk from the bucket into dairy product containers, such as yogurt, cottage cheese, milk, butter tubs, and so on. Ask the children to think of other animals on the farm and paint those as well.

The animals will need some hay to eat! Provide paper grocery bags to make hay as some children may be allergic to the real thing. Stuff brown paper grocery bags with newspaper and tape them shut, using them for hay bails, or provide the children with brown boxes for them to paint to resemble a hay bail. Provide brown and yellow markers to draw the hay on the sides of the boxes. Bind with twine.

Many farms have chickens that provide fresh eggs. Make chicken nesting boxes by using shoe boxes with shredded brown paper or newspaper for nesting hay. Place white and brown plastic eggs in the boxes for young farmers to collect each morning. Don't forget the basket for gathering up the eggs! Once the eggs have been gathered, provide egg cartons to store the eggs.

Create a farmer's vegetable garden by using 4" to 6" thick upholstery foam, about the size of a chair seat cushion or larger. Using adult scissors the teacher should cut slits into the sheet of foam so plastic root vegetables (potatoes, carrots, beets) can be tucked into the foam "ground," waiting to be harvested. Give gardeners a small plastic hand trowel and basket to dig up their bounty and carry the food back to the farm house.

After the eggs have been collected, the cows have been milked, and the vegetables have been picked, have children set up a roadside stand to sell their goods. A free standing puppet theater turns into a farmer's roadside stand. Signs on the roadside stand will let the customers know what is for sale and how much each item costs. Supply empty grocery bags for customers to carry their purchases home.

- What do you think grows on a farm?
- How does the farm get their produce to the market?
- How do the animals sleep at night?
- How will you keep the eggs and milk fresh?

Literacy Connections

Songs and Fingerplays

Ten Little Hens, a poem

Have children stand when they recite this poem.

Ten little hens went strutting in their pen. *(Hold up ten fingers.)*
They ruffled their feathers so. *(Flap your wings.)*
They scratched on the ground and pecked at the earth. *(Use your feet to scratch at the ground.)*
Looking for some food below. *(Search the floor for some food.)*

They pecked at a worm and a tiny little bug. *(Use your hand like the beak of a chicken to peck.)*
But they liked the corn meal best. *(Big smile!)*
They ate and they ate till their bellies were full. *(Rub your tummies.)*
Then they all went back to their nest. *(Sit down.)*

Five Little Chickens Sitting in Their Nest

Use the pattern on the **CD** to make the five little chicken finger puppets.

Five little chickens sitting in their nest.
The first one said, "My egg's the best."
The second one said, "My egg's so round."
The third one said, "Mine dropped to the ground!"
The fourth one said, "Girls, let's not fight."
The fifth one said, "It's time to say good night."
They all closed their eyes, and they went to sleep,
Listening to the "baaing" of their friends the wooly sheep.

Down on the Farm

(Sing to the tune "Down by the Bay.")

Down on the Farm
Where the roosters crow
Back to their stalls
The animals go
And Farmer Brown
Asked with a frown,

"Did you ever see a hen writing with a pen, down on the farm?"
"Did you ever see a cow taking a bow, down on the farm?"
"Did you ever see a pig dancing a jig, down on the farm?"
"Did you ever see a mare going to the fair, down on the farm?"
"Did you ever see a sheep driving a jeep, down on the farm?"
"Did you ever see a goat floating in a boat, down on the farm?"

Vocabulary Builders

New Words and Word Study: Reinforce the names for various farm animals such as *goats, sheep, horses, cows, chickens, hens, roosters,* and *pigs.* Find pictures of these animals and put them up in the classroom with the animal name written next to the picture. Other words to use: *crops, produce, vegetables, tractor, barn, pen, corral, silo, hay, barnyard,* and *roadside stand.*

Onset/Rime: Words that have the same spelling pattern as the word *hen*.

/en/ den, hen, men, pen, ten, when, then

Write All About It!

Down on the Farm Class Book

Have children dictate or write about an animal they would like to have on their own farm. Begin with the predictable text, *Down on (child's name) farm there was a/an (animal name).* Use barn shaped paper for this class book. Ask children to illustrate the animal they have named. Make the cover out of red construction paper in the shape of a barn.

Book List

- *Biscuit Visits the Farm,* by Alyssa Satin Capucilli
- *Big Red Barn,* by Margaret Wise Brown
- *If You Give a Pig a Pancake,* by Laura Joffe Numeroff
- *All the Places to Love,* by Patricia MacLachlan
- *Moo Who?,* by Margie Palatini
- *Day at Greenhill Farm,* by Sue Nicholson
- *Barn Cat: A Counting Book,* by Carol P. Saul, Mary Azarian
- *Serious Farm,* by Tim Egan
- *Farm Alphabet Book,* by Jane Miller
- *Beatrice's Goat,* by Page McBrier
- *Rosie's Walk,* by Pat Hutchins
- *Click, Clack, Moo: Cows That Type,* by Doreen Cronin, Betsy Lewin
- *Giggle, Giggle, Quack,* by Doreen Cronin, Betsy Lewin
- *The Rusty, Trusty Tractor,* by Joy Cowley, Olivier Dunrea
- *Barn Dance!,* by Bill Martin Jr, John Archambault

Down on the Farm (The End)

Dramatic Creations: Let's Take a Walk

Taking a page from the book *Rosie's Walk* by Pat Hutchins, children in this guided drama will walk through the barnyard, overcoming some obstacles along the way. The narrator directs the action as the children go on their walk through the barnyard.

Lay out an obstacle course in the center of the room. Place a blue tarp or vinyl tablecloth to represent a small pond, milking buckets for children to weave through, a small bail of hay, two chairs about 3 feet apart positioned back to back with a towel stretched over them to create a bridge to duck under, and a large cardboard box with both ends open so children can crawl through.

Narrator: *(Child's name)* the *(animal name)* went out for a walk. He/She swam through the water *(blue tarp)*, went around the buckets, jumped over the hay, ducked under the bridge, and crawled through the rain barrel. Then *(child's name)* the *(animal name)* went back home for a long rest. *(Child sits back in the circle.)*

The action continues as each child each gets a turn to walk through the barnyard. Write each of the action phrases on sentence strips and put them in a pocket chart. As the action is repeated over and over again, encourage children to chant along. Use a pointer as the script is read or recited. Ask one child if he or she would like to use the pointer and be the narrator.

Encourage children to think of different obstacles that they could encounter on subsequent walks through the barnyard and how that obstacle might be made. Work collaboratively to gather materials and write a new script.

Rearrange the sentence strips so the action is different each time. To help children read the script, place pictures on the sentence strips.

1-57029-533-6 *Year 'Round Dramatic Play*

An Apple a Day

Props and Supplies

lengths of blue and brown felt, felt scraps (pink, white, red, yellow, green, orange), scissors, hot glue, Velcro, curtain rod or 1/2" dowel, cord, felt or artificial bees, plastic apples, baskets, clean plastic applesauce and apple juice containers, pie tins, free standing puppet theater, play money, cash register, and grocery bags

Setting the Stage

Tending an apple orchard is a year-round business. Even though the focus in this section is on the harvest in autumn, children will still experience the cyclical nature of apples as they tend to their orchard through dramatic play. Create a large felt tree banner using blue felt as the background. Sew or hot glue on a bare-branched, brown felt tree to this backdrop. The tree should be sizeable, yet not so tall that young children can't reach the top branches.

Hang the tree on a wall using a sturdy curtain rod or dowel (1/2" or larger diameter). Use a length of cord tied to both ends of the rod or dowel to create a banner hanger. A nail in the wall gives you a place to hang the fall tree banner. If you have a sizeable bulletin board, use push pins or staples to secure the tree scene there.

Once the tree is up, use felt props to enact the year of the tree. Cut little pink or white apple blossoms from felt scraps, or purchase small artificial flowers. Honeybees are a necessary part of the apples life cycle. Purchase artificial bees or create your own using felt scraps. Big green felt leaves add a summer's touch.

Hang ripe apples from the tree in the autumn. Provide a variety of felt apples for them to "grow" on their tree. Use red, light green, and yellow felt scraps to make apples of varying sizes. Don't forget the fall foliage! Make red, yellow, orange, and brown felt leaves of different sizes to reflect the season.

Once the fruit is picked from the class apple tree, the action moves into the housekeeping area. Have children make yummy pretend treats with their harvest. Provide plastic apples, clean plastic applesauce jars, and plastic apple juice containers for them to use. Pie tins will spur the little bakers on to make pies for themselves and their friends.

Give children the opportunity to sell the apples and their baked goods at a little market. Use a free standing puppet theater for the shopkeeper to sell his or her apple goodies. Add play money and a cash register. Have some grocery bags available to package the items purchased by customers.

- What will you do with all of the apples you pick?
- I wonder why there are different colors of apples.
- Do you think that all apples taste the same?
- How will you sort the apples you pick?

Literacy Connections

Songs and Fingerplays

Ten Little Apples
(Sing to the tune "Ten Little Indians.")

One little, two little, three little apples,
Four little, five little, six little apples,
Seven little, eight little, nine little apples,
Ten apples on the tree.

We picked the apples and made a pie.
We picked the apples and made a pie.
We picked the apples and made a pie.
All on an autumn day.

(Substitute other apple goodies for "pie," such as applesauce, apple butter, apple cider, apple juice.)

I Saw an Apple
(Sing to the tune "Hush Little Baby.")

I saw an apple on the tree,
The biggest one I ever did see!
A pie is what I made for me.
Now I'm a full as I can be.

I saw an apple on the tree
The biggest one I ever did see!
A fritter is what I made for me.
Now I'm as full as I can be.

(Create other verses for *I Saw an Apple* using food products made from apples such as applesauce, apple cider, apple cake, apple crisp, apple juice, and so on.)

Five Little Apples
Use the apple pattern on the (CD) to make finger puppets for this finger play.

Five little apples hanging way up high.
A baker came by and said, "I'll make some pie."
The wind blew hard and shook the branches so,
That the angry baker said, "I think I'll have to go."

Five little apples in the morning sun.
A worm came by and said, "I'll have some fun!"
The wind blew hard and shook the branches so,
That the wiggly little worm said, "I think I'll have
   to go."

Five little apples growing on the tree.
A boy came by and said, "Here's one for me."
The wind blew hard and shook the branches so,
That the little boy said, "I think I'll have to go."

The five little apples were safe on the tree.
They all gave a smile and said with glee,
"Thank you, Mr. Wind, for blowing very hard!
We're safe as can be, in our tree, in the yard."

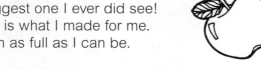

Vocabulary Builders

New Words and Word Study: Children will probably be familiar with apples, but other terms related to their growing and picking may not be as familiar. Focus on those words such as *blossom, harvest, orchard, picker, peel, core, branches, limbs, cider,* and *cider press.*

Onset/Rime: Words that have the same spelling pattern as the word *day.*

/ay/ bay, day, hay, pay, ray, say, may, lay, way, tray, stray

Write All About It!

The Apple Café Class Book

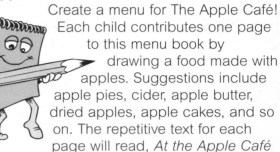

Create a menu for The Apple Café! Each child contributes one page to this menu book by drawing a food made with apples. Suggestions include apple pies, cider, apple butter, dried apples, apple cakes, and so on. The repetitive text for each page will read, *At the Apple Café you can order _____.* Each child dictates or writes the food item they have chosen and then they illustrate that food item on their page.

Book List

- *Apple Picking Time,* by Michele Benoit Slawson
- *Autumn Is for Apples,* by Michelle Knudsen
- *Picking Apples and Pumpkins,* by Amy Hutchings, Richard Hutchings
- *Ten Red Apples,* by Pat Hutchins
- *I Am an Apple,* by Jean Marzollo, Judith Moffatt
- *Russ and the Apple Tree Surprise,* by Janet Elizabeth Rickert
- *Picking Apples,* by Gail Saunders-Smith
- *Apples and How They Grow,* by Laura Driscoll, Tammy Smith
- *Up, up, up!: It's Apple-Picking Time,* by Jody Fickes Shapiro, Kitty Harvill
- *Apple Cider Making Days,* by Ann Purmell
- *The Apple Pie Tree,* by Zoe Hall, Shari Halpern
- *Apples,* by Gail Gibbons
- *Applesauce,* by Shirley Kurtz, Cheryl Benner
- *Down the Road,* by Alice Schertle
- *Johnny Appleseed,* by Stephen Benet
- *Apple Valley Year,* by Ann Turner
- *The Seasons of Arnold's Apple Tree,* by Gail Gibbons

An Apple a Day (The End)

Dramatic Creations: Apple-Picking Time

It's time to go out into the orchard and pick some apples! In groups of three, ask children to go into the pretend orchard to pick apples. The pattern of the script will remind children of another familiar story as they search for apples that are just right!

Narrator: One day, three friends went out into the apple orchard. They were looking for some yummy apples to make some treats.

Child #1: These apples are too small.

Child # 2: These apples are too big.

Child #3: These apples are just right. I think I'll make some pie. *(Children pretend to pick apples.)*

Narrator: So the three friends went back to their house and made some apple pie. The next day they went out into the orchard again to look for some more yummy apples to make some treats.

Child #1: These apples are too soft.

Child #2: These apples are too hard.

Child #3: These apples are just right. I think I'll make some apple dumplings. *(Children pretend to pick apples.)*

Narrator: So the three friends went back to their house and made some apple dumplings. The next day they went out into the orchard again to look for some more yummy apples to make some treats.

Child #1: These apples are too sour.

Child #2: These apples are too sweet.

Child #3: These apples are just right. I think I'll make some apple cider. *(Children pretend to pick apples.)*

Narrator: So the three friends went back to their house and made some apple cider. The next day they went out into the orchard again to look for some more yummy apples to make some treats. They came upon a tall apple tree with many delicious, juicy, ripe, red apples. Just as they were reaching up to pick some, they heard a big, gruff voice.

Bear: Who's that picking my apples?

Narrator: The children all turned around and saw a big bear! They were so frightened they ran back to their house and locked the door. The bear looked sad.

Bear: I didn't want to frighten them away. I just wanted someone to eat my apples with!

The Falling Leaves

Props and Supplies

rolls of butcher paper, tempera paint (red, green, yellow, orange, brown), sponges cut in leaf shapes, construction paper, tissue paper, white school glue, paintbrushes, small wooden bushel baskets, child-sized wheelbarrow, plastic rakes, silk leaves, acorns or other nuts in their shells, small fan, and plush squirrels

Setting the Stage

Let the autumn fun begin by playing with brightly colored, freshly fallen leaves from the trees! Have children begin by creating a forest of autumn trees in the classroom using large pieces of butcher paper and paint. Using several pieces of 6' high lengths of paper, ask children to paint the tree trunks. Provide an outline for them to follow. Once the tree trunks are dry, add the leaves! There are several ways to do this. Use one, two, or all three methods listed below. Compare the results!

Leaf Method One: Cut sponges into various leaf shapes. Evenly dip into tempera paint, and then print the leaf shape onto the painted branches.

Leaf Method Two: Have children use torn construction paper or colored tissue paper to represent the leaves on the trees. Provide real leaves for them to use as models. Help them to make small, controlled tears in the paper. Once the construction paper leaves are torn, apply glue to the backs, and position them onto the tree branches. If using tissue paper, make a thin white glue wash (3 parts glue to 1 part water). Apply a thin coat of glue wash to the background paper, then place the torn tissue paper on top.

Leaf Method Three: Directly glue silk or real leaves onto the branches of your painted tree!

Securely attach the autumn trees to a wall in the classroom. Once the backdrop is in place, begin to add other props. Bring in small wooden bushel baskets, child-sized wheelbarrows, and plastic rakes for children to keep their autumn yard clean. Use silk fall leaves for this activity as freshly fallen real leaves will dry and crumble. Be cautious in using real leaves in the classroom as some children may have allergies. Purchase garlands of autumn leaves from a craft store and then cut the leaves off. Scatter the leaves in the autumn tree corner of the classroom. Add a few acorns or other nuts in their shells to the mix as well. Complete the autumnal scene by adding a few plush squirrels. Use a small fan, safely out of the children's reach, to simulate the wind blowing leaves all around!

1-57029-533-6 *Year 'Round Dramatic Play*

The Falling Leaves (cont.)

• What will you do with the leaves once you've raked them?
• Why do you think the leaves fall off the trees?
• I wonder why the leaves are all different colors.
• What do you think will happen to the acorns that have fallen?

Literacy Connections

Songs and Fingerplays

Leaves Are Falling

Leaves are falling to the ground. *(Raise hands high in the air, then flutter your fingers as you slowly lower your arms.)*
Leaves are swirling round and round. *(Make swirling motions with both hands on the floor.)*
Leaves piled in a great big mound. *(Raise arms above your head to make a circle.)*
Look at all the leaves I found! *(Use one hand, held over your eyes like a visor, to "see" all of the leaves that were found.)*

Where Is Red Leaf?

(Sing to the tune "Where Is Thumbkin?")

Guide children in making leaf finger puppets using the pattern on the ⬤.

Where is red leaf, where is red leaf?
Here I am, here I am.
Bright and shiny red leaf,
Falling to the ground leaf.
Blown around, blown around.

Where is orange leaf, where is orange leaf?
Here I am, here I am.
Bright and shiny orange leaf,
Falling to the ground leaf.
Blown around, blown around.

(Continue with other fall colors.)

Leaves

(Sing to the tune "Twinkle, Twinkle Little Star.")

Leaves on the green grass,
Leaves on the road,
Leaves on the hill side,
Leaves on the toad!

Leaves on the pumpkins,
Leaves on the trees,
Leaves on the sidewalk,
Leaves on ME!

Leaves are falling to the ground.
Watch them swirling round and round.

Vocabulary Builders

New Words and Word Study: Seasonal changes may not be as apparent in  certain parts of the country. In the northern climates, however, the changes in the scenery and weather are abundantly clear! Help children to understand the changes in the earth by emphasizing these words: *seasons*, *leaves*, *autumn*, *rake*, *bushel baskets*, *wheelbarrow*, *wind*, *breeze*, *tree trunk*, *branches*, *tree limbs*, *chilly*, and *frost*.

Onset/Rime: Words that have the same spelling pattern as the word *fall*.

/all/ *ball, call, fall, hall, tall, wall, all*

Write All About It!

Busy Squirrels Class Book

Have children use their imaginations to think of hiding places that squirrels might use to store up their winter food. The repetitive text in this class book will read, *A little squirrel hid a nut. He hid it in a(an) _____.* Children dictate or write the completion of that sentence. Encourage them to think of unusual and interesting places for their little squirrel to hide a nut. Ask children to draw an illustration to accompany their text.

Leaves Class Book

Use the text pattern in "Leaves" from *Songs and Fingerplay* section to create the predictable text for this class book. Each child writes a page with the text, *Leaves on_____.* Have children name an item on which leaves will have fallen, and illustrate accordingly.

Book List

- *Fall Leaves Fall!*, by Zoe Hall, Shari Halpern
- *Autumn Leaves*, by Gail Saunders-Smith
- *I Am a Leaf*, by Jean Marzollo, Judith Moffatt
- *Plant Leaves*, by David M. Schwartz, Dwight Kuhn
- *Autumn Story*, by Jill Barklem
- *Autumn: An Alphabet Acrostic*, by Steven Schnur
- *When Autumn Comes*, by Robert Maass
- *Every Autumn Comes the Bear*, by Jim Arnosky
- *Best Fall of All*, by Laura Godwin
- *Animals in the Fall*, by Gail Saunders-Smith
- *Lily and Trooper's Fall*, by Jung-Hee Spetter
- *The Wind Blew*, by Pat Hutchins
- *Squirrels and Chipmunks*, by Allan Fowler
- *Squirrels*, by Brian Wildsmith
- *A Squirrel's Tale*, by Richard Fowler
- *Gray Squirrel's Daring Day*, by Geri Harrington

The Falling Leaves (The End)

Dramatic Creations: Blow, Wind, Blow

In this drama activity, children take on the roles of the wind and fallen leaves. Divide children into three groups: the north wind, the south wind, and the fallen leaves. The north and south winds sit in parallel lines, opposite from one another, and a good distance apart. You will need plenty of room in the middle for the fallen leaves! The leaves begin by standing between the two lines of "wind."

Narrator: Autumn is here. The nights are cooler. The leaves on the trees are turning colors. One by one the leaves fall to the ground. *(Leaves gently "fall" to the ground one at a time. The leaves lay straight with their arms extended above their heads. They position their bodies so they are parallel to the north and south winds.)*

Narrator: Soon the north wind began to blow a gentle breeze. *(North wind blows gently toward the leaves. The leaves do one barrel roll away from the north wind towards the children who are the south wind. The north wind stops blowing.)*

Narrator: Then the south wind began to blow a gentle breeze. *(South wind blows gently toward the leaves. The leaves do one barrel roll towards the north and away from the south. The south wind stops blowing.)*

Narrator: The north wind began to blow a little stronger. *(North wind blows. The leaves do two barrel rolls away from the north wind and towards the south wind. The north wind stops blowing.)*

Narrator: Then the south wind began to blow a little stronger. *(Similar action in north.)*

Narrator: The north wind began to blow even stronger. *(The action continues as indicated above with the leaves doing three barrel rolls.)*

Narrator: Then the south wind began to blow even stronger. *(The action continues as indicated above with the leaves doing three barrel rolls.)*

Narrator: The north wind began to blow very strong.

Narrator: Then the south wind began to blow very strong, too. And the little fallen leaves are blown away! *(Leaf children stand and leave.)*

Rotate the three groups so all children have an opportunity to be the fallen, tumbling leaves.

Props and Supplies

brown paper bags of varying sizes, newspaper, tempera paint (orange, green, and brown), rubber bands, green nylon rope, green construction paper, spring-action clothes pins, blankets, large cardboard pieces, horse masks from the pattern on the 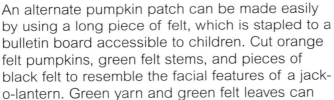, large piece of blue felt, felt squares (orange, green and black), and green yarn

Setting the Stage

A visit to the pumpkin patch is a typical annual event for some young children. Create the experience in the classroom by bringing in some real pumpkins for them to use in their play. Select pumpkins that are in varying sizes and small enough so young children can carry them easily.

Create pretend pumpkins using brown paper bags of varying sizes such as grocery bags or lunch bags. Stuff the paper bags with newspaper almost to the top of the bag. Close the bag using rubber bands tied about 2" to 3" below the top of the bag. That creates the stem which the children will paint green. The rest of the bag is painted orange to resemble the real pumpkin.

Pumpkins grow on a vine. Use green nylon rope to duplicate this part of the plant. Use spring-action clothes pins to secure the paper pumpkins onto the rope. Have children add green leaves to the vine by cutting leaf shapes from green construction paper and taping them to the vine.

An alternate pumpkin patch can be made easily by using a long piece of felt, which is stapled to a bulletin board accessible to children. Cut orange felt pumpkins, green felt stems, and pieces of black felt to resemble the facial features of a jack-o-lantern. Green yarn and green felt leaves can be arranged in any way the children desire on this large felt pumpkin patch.

A visit to the pumpkin patch isn't complete without a hayride! Have children transform a rectangular classroom table into a hay wagon. Cover the table with comfy blankets. Using large pieces of cardboard cut into circles, ask children to make the wheels for this wagon. With paintbrushes, have children begin in the center of the wheel and paint spokes outward towards the rim. A rim for the wheel can easily be added with additional brush strokes. Secure the dried wheels to the sides of the table using sturdy tape.

When children are riding on the hay wagon, emphasize safety. Have them sit on the edge of the table while riding into the pumpkin patch. Recruit a couple of work horses to "pull" the wagon on its way. Use the pattern on the 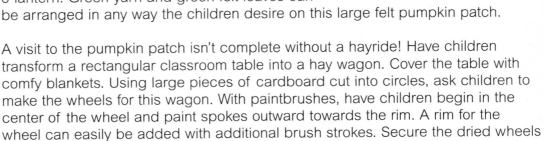 to make horse masks.

While on their trip to the pumpkin patch, children gather up the pumpkins they've created. Next, the play shifts to the art center where the children decorate their pumpkins for autumn. Suggest that they add jack-o-lantern faces expressing various emotions, or use their imaginations to create the decorations of their choice. Paint either the real pumpkins or the paper bag pumpkins, or both!

Teacher Talk

- I wonder what's inside of real pumpkins.
- Do you think that a pumpkin can float?
- I wonder how they make pies out of pumpkins.
- Are pumpkins always orange?

Literacy Connections

Songs and Fingerplays

Have You Seen the Pumpkin Patch?
(Sing to the tune "The Muffin Man.")

Have you seen the pumpkin patch,
The pumpkin patch, the pumpkin patch?
Have you seen the pumpkin patch,
That grows behind the barn?

Oh yes, I've seen the pumpkin patch,
The pumpkin patch, the pumpkin patch.
Yes, I've seen the pumpkin patch,
That grows behind the barn!

Sing other verses with different positions and locations such as:
    That grows next to the house
    That grows in my backyard
    That grows beside the fence
    That grows under the tree

I'm a Great Big Pumpkin
(Sing to the tune "I'm a Little Teapot.")

I'm a great big pumpkin, orange and round.
I grew from a seed that was planted in the ground.
Now its time to pick me to make a pie,
Or a jack-o-lantern with big bright eyes.

Pumpkins

Pumpkins growing on a vine,
Pumpkins orange and round.
Pumpkins looking very fine,
Growing on the ground.

Pumpkins are for making pies,
Pumpkins full of seeds.
Pumpkins with a light inside,
Just for you and me!

Literacy Connections (cont.)

Vocabulary Builders

New Words and Word Study: It takes a lot of room to grow pumpkins in the family garden. Therefore, some children may not be familiar with what they look like while growing. Emphasize words that deal with the structure of pumpkins as well as how they grow. Words to use: *pumpkin, squash, round, sphere, jack-o-lantern, pulp, seeds, vine, pumpkin patch, orange, stem,* and *purchase.* Often pumpkins grow to very large sizes. Use synonyms for *big,* such as *huge, enormous, giant, gigantic,* and so on.

Onset/Rime: Words that have the same spelling pattern as the word *vine.*

/ine/ dine, fine, line, mine, nine, vine

Write All About It!

Pumpkins As Big As... Class Book

Create a humorous class book as children think about super-sized pumpkins! The text for this book reads, *(Child's name) grew a pumpkin as large as a/an _____.* Have children dictate or write the completion of the sentence. In illustrating their text, have children draw their larger than life pumpkin in that context. For example, a pumpkin as large as a car will be drawn to resemble a car with four wheels, radio antenna, head lights, and so on. A pumpkin as large as a house will have a front door, windows, a chimney, and so on.

Book List

- *The Biggest Pumpkin Ever*, by Steven Kroll, Jeni Bassett
- *From Seed to Pumpkin*, by Wendy Pfeffer
- *From Seed to Pumpkin (Welcome Books)*, by Jan Kottke
- *Garden That We Grew*, by Joan Holub
- *In Search of the Perfect Pumpkin*, by Gloria Evangelista, Shawn Shea
- *One Child, One Seed: A South African Counting Book*, by Kathryn Cave
- *Pumpkin Day, Pumpkin Night*, by Anne Rockwell, Megan Halsey
- *Pumpkin Pumpkin*, by Jeanne Titherington
- *Snow Pumpkin*, by Carole Lexa Schaefer
- *Too Many Pumpkins*, by Linda White, Megan Lloyd
- *The Pumpkin Book*, by Gail Gibbons
- *The Pumpkin Patch*, by Elizabeth King

Pumpkin Patch (The End)

Dramatic Creations: Jack-o-lanterns for Sale

Ask children to pretend to be customers who want to purchase jack-o-lanterns that are "just right"! The jack-o-lanterns will be played by actors wearing jack-o-lantern masks, created by using the pattern on the **CD**. Guide the children in having the jack-o-lanterns represent a variety of facial expressions: happy, sad, angry, surprised, sleepy, scary, and so on.

(Three jack-o-lanterns are waiting in line for the customer to enter the store.)

Narrator: One day a girl went to the store to purchase a jack-o-lantern. She looked at the first jack-o-lantern and said,

Child #1: This jack-o-lantern is too…. *(Describe the facial expression of the first jack-o-lantern actor.)*

Narrator: She went to the second jack-o-lantern and said,

Child #1: This jack-o-lantern is too…. *(Describes the facial expression of the second jack-o-lantern actor.)*

Narrator: Then she went to the third jack-o-lantern and said,

Child #1: This jack-o-lantern is just right.

Narrator: So, she purchased that jack-o-lantern and took it home. *(The first three jack-o-lanterns and Child #1 leave the scene. Three different jack-o-lanterns enter the scene.)*

Narrator: A little later a boy went to the store to purchase a jack-o-lantern. He looked at the first jack-o-lantern and said,

Child #2: This jack-o-lantern is too…. *(Describe the facial expression of the fist jack-o-lantern actor.)*

Narrator: He went to the second jack-o-lantern and said,

Child #2: This jack-o-lantern is too…. *(Describe the facial expression of the second jack-o-lantern actor.)*

Narrator: Then he went to the third jack-o-lantern and said,

Child #2: This jack-o-lantern is just right.

Narrator: So, he purchased that jack-o-lantern and took it home.

(The play continues until all of the children have had a chance to be a part of this drama, either as a customer or a pumpkin actor.)

The Costume Ball

Setting the Stage

The mainstay of pretend play for many young children is in dressing up. Putting on fancy, grown-up clothing invites the young imagination to dream of royalty and castles, fancy balls, and fairyland adventures.

Props and Supplies

prom or wedding dresses, crowns, gloves, beaded purses, veils, tuxedos, bow ties, crowns, silk flowers for corsages and boutonnières, florist tape, safety pins, classical music (such as waltzes), wagons, streamers, scarves, jewelry, full-length mirror, parchment paper, envelopes, self-sticking gold seals, 1" ribbon scraps, serving trays, doilies, punch bowl with serving ladle, punch cups, and costume masks

Begin by building a treasure chest of dress-up clothes fit for a king or queen. Gently used prom dresses, bridesmaid dresses, wedding dresses and veils, and tuxedos with bow ties provide the foundation for a fancy evening ball. To that add fancy shoes for boys and girls, gloves and beaded purses, jewelry, veils, and crowns. Provide full-length mirrors for the children.

To help children move with ease in their dress-up clothes, pay attention to lengths of hemlines and sleeves and make alterations as needed. Shorten gowns by cutting off the bottom portion and re-hemming the garment. Don't discard the extra fabric. Turn it into a matching shawl. Finish the outfit with elegant jewelry, bedazzling crowns, and flowers.

Make corsages and boutonnières out of silk flowers taped together using florist tape. A large safety pin will hold the corsage or boutonnières in place. Turn the corsage into a wrist corsage with a short piece of elastic made into a wrist band.

Ask children to invite each other to the ball by writing invitations and "mailing" them to their classmates. Provide parchment paper and envelopes for the invitations. Self-sticking gold seals with ribbon attached make them look official. Set the time and the day for the ball and allow plenty of time to play dress up before the culminating event.

Have children decorate wagons as coaches to pick up the guests and transport them to the ballroom. Once there, they will dance to the tunes of waltzes and dine on little tea sandwiches served on doily-laced trays. A punch bowl adds a festive touch to the glamour of the party.

An alternative to a fancy ball is a masquerade party. Add costumes and appropriate props to the dress-up collection so young children can have many experiences dressing up in different types of clothing. With costumes, they have the opportunity to take on different roles for pretend play such as animals, fire fighters, doctors, clowns and so on.

Sometimes young children can become frightened of masks. By providing friendly masks for them to play with, children can become more familiar with how masks work. Who's behind that mask? It's only me!

- If your face is covered by a mask, how else will your friends know that it's you?
- I wonder how you feel when you wear that costume.
- What kinds of food will you have at the costume ball?
- Have you been practicing your dancing?

Literacy Connections

Songs and Fingerplays

Dancing
(Sing to the tune "Here We Go Round the Mulberry Bush.")

Have children dance the corresponding motions to this action song.

We're dancing very fast today, fast today, fast today.
We're dancing very fast today at the costume ball.

Other verses:
We're dancing very slow today.
We're dancing in a circle today.
We're dancing with a partner today.
We're dancing on one foot today.
We're dancing round and round today.

When I Look into the Mirror
Guide children in creating paper-plate masks to use in this poem. Select two children to stand while reciting this poem and insert the type of mask they are wearing into the blank spaces. For example it might read, A *lion* or *tiger* or *something more*? Write the words to the poem on sentence strips and prepare word cards to be inserted in the blanks to increase word recognition.

When I look into the mirror,
What do you think I see?
A _____ or _____ or something more?
No, I just see me!

I Wrote an Invitation
(Sing to the tune "The Eensy Weensy Spider.")

I wrote an invitation
To the costume ball.
It wasn't very wide
And it wasn't very tall.
It told the place and time
And the costume to wear.
It went out to the letter box
For all my friends to share.

Vocabulary Builders

New Words and Word Study: Castles and royalty invite the imagination to dream of splendor. Focus on words as regal as their costumes such as *glamorous, glittery, flowing, splendid, elegant, handsome, dashing, gowns, corsage, boutonnière, masquerade, ball, ballroom, carriage, waltz,* and *dance partner.*

Onset/Rime: Words that have the same spelling pattern as the word *clap.*
/ap/ *cap, lap, nap, tap, clap, snap, map, trap, flap*

Write All About It!

Invitations to the Ball

Guide children in writing invitations to the fancy ball or the masquerade ball by using the template on the CD. Have them create a drawing on the cover and provide the following information on the inside: time, place, and what to wear. Seal the invitations with gold self-sticking medallions. Assign children one classmate to send their invitation to. Use classroom cubbies as mailboxes.

Who's Behind That Mask? Class Book

Help children understand that masks are for fun and that someone they know might be hiding behind one! This class book requires some assembly. Each child creates one page with this text at the top of the page, *Behind the _____ mask was...* Children dictate or write the type of mask in the blank space. Below that phrase, ask them to draw a self portrait with their name written nearby. Put this drawing underneath a mask created by the child, using the template on the CD. The mask may be of anything! For example, a tiger mask with orange and black stripes might cover the self portrait of the child. The mask will be taped along one side, so the children can flip the page open revealing the author and illustrator.

Book List

- *Costume Ball*, by Katharine Holabird, Barbara Slade, Helen Craig
- *Dressing Up with Mr. Bumble*, by John Wallace
- *Spot Goes to a Party*, by Eric Hill
- *Maisy Dresses Up*, by Lucy Cousins
- *My Day in the Garden*, by Miela Ford
- *What Can I Be?*, by Cari Meister
- *Nino's Mask*, by Jeanette Winter
- *Little Bear Makes a Mask*, by Else Holmelund Minarik
- *Carl's Masquerade*, by Alexandra Day
- *Cinderella*: There are many versions of this timeless tale, some are set in different cultures and in different times. Select the versions that seem most appropriate for your children.

The Costume Ball (The End)

Dramatic Creations: The Animal Masquerade Party

Children are invited to a masquerade party; however, each forgets his or her costume! Select several children to be the guests. Have them stand in a line waiting their turn to enter the circle. Select one child to be the host or hostess. Make cue cards with different animal names on them, which will be the animal costume to be acted out.

The host or hostess introduces each guest by saying, "*May I introduce (child's name) who is wearing…*" The guest enters the circle and responds with an imitation of the animal costume given on a cue card shown to him or her by the teacher. The children in the circle try to guess what animal the guest is acting out.

Dramatic Creations: The Fancy Ball

All children participate in acting out this fairy-tale ball! Provide a large supply of costume accessories such as veils, gloves, shoes, purses, jewelry, corsages, boutonnières, hats, and so on. Place them in a prop box or on the floor in the center of the circle, so they are easily accessible to all the children. Have children sit and move in a circle during the drama. The teacher or narrator makes and then reads invitations that contain directions for the children to act out. After the drama, put the invitations into the fancy ball prop box for children to have an opportunity to use on their own.

Narrator: *(Opens an invitation and reads…)* You are invited to a fancy ball. Please wear something special. *(Allow a few children at a time to go to the prop box to get their special accessory. One way is to select children by the color they are wearing. You might say…* "If you are wearing something red, you may select something special to wear to the fancy ball." *Or* "If you are wearing something green, you may select something special to wear to the fancy ball." *The narrator continues until all children have selected something from the fancy ball props.)*

Narrator: *(Opens a second invitation and reads…)* Your carriage awaits you. Please step in and let the horses take you to the ball. *(Children gallop like horses in a large circle, moving in the same direction.)*

Narrator: *(Opens a third invitation and reads…)* Welcome to the fancy ballroom. Listen to the music play. You are invited to join the dance. *(A waltz is played and children dance in the circle.)*

Narrator: *(Opens a fourth invitation and reads…)* For your enjoyment, refreshments are now being served. Please enjoy the punch and cookies. *(Children stop dancing and pretend to drink punch and eat cookies.)*

Narrator: *(Opens a fifth invitation and reads…)* Thank you for coming to the fancy ball. Your carriages await to take you home. *(Children gallop like horses again, moving in the circle going in the opposite direction as they travel home.)*

Narrator: *(Opens a sixth invitation and reads…)* Welcome home. Now it is time for a little rest. *(Children remove their fancy ball prop, returning it to the prop box. They go back to their place in the circle and lay down for a little nap.)*

Pepperoni, Please!

Props and Supplies

free standing puppet theater, play dough, rolling pins, pizza pans, red felt circles cut in 6", 8", and 10" diameters, felt scraps (grey, green, brown, red, yellow, and black for the pizza toppings), off-white yarn for pizza cheese, pizza boxes, cardboard rounds, white aprons, bakers caps, small child-sized tables and chairs, red checkered tablecloth, plastic vases, artificial flowers, waiter aprons, picture menus, picture order slips, pencils, phones, wagon, cash register, and play money

Setting the Stage

What's for dinner? Pizza! Help children turn the housekeeping area into a busy pizzeria, making and baking these delicious pies for themselves and their friends to enjoy. Begin by making several large batches of play dough. No need to color the dough since it's just the right shade! Provide children with a table surface to roll the dough with large rolling pins. Once the dough is just the right size, transfer it to round pizza pans for the next phase in pizza making. Make several circles from red felt for the sauce. Cut out small (6"), medium (8"), and large (10") saucy circles for the chefs to use.

Top the pizzas according to the customers' orders. In setting up the props for this unit of dramatic play, brainstorm the possible toppings that children might order. Use scrap felt pieces to cut mushrooms, green peppers, ham, pepperoni, pineapple, olives, and other favorite toppings. Top off the pizzas with "shreds" of off-white colored yarn cut into 1" pieces for the cheese. Add to the recipe some real pizza boxes and cardboard rounds and the pizzeria is just about ready to open for business! Dress the bakers in white aprons with baker's caps, and they will look the part!

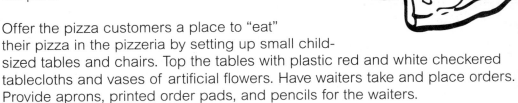

Offer the pizza customers a place to "eat" their pizza in the pizzeria by setting up small child-sized tables and chairs. Top the tables with plastic red and white checkered tablecloths and vases of artificial flowers. Have waiters take and place orders. Provide aprons, printed order pads, and pencils for the waiters.

Create a menu out of pictures. The diners select their toppings for their pizzas and the waiter will mark off those toppings on the paper order slip before handing it to the chef through the puppet theater divide. The chef reads the order and makes a custom-ordered pizza. Once the pizza is ready the chef alerts the waiter and then passes the pizza through the puppet theater divide. The waiter presents the bill to the customers who use play money to pay for their delicious dinner.

Carry out? You bet! Have several phones handy so orders can be called in to the pizzeria. Have the pizza delivery person drive the pizza right to the customer's door using a wagon to hold the "hot" dinner. Don't forget to leave a tip!

• I wonder what the favorite pizza topping is in this class.
• How will the delivery person keep the pizza "hot" until it reaches the customer?
• How will you keep the ingredients fresh until the pizzeria opens again tomorrow?
• Have you ever heard of putting fish on a pizza?

Literacy Connections

Songs and Fingerplays

Toss the Dough
(Sing to the tune "London Bridge.")

Children will act out the motions as singing this song.

Toss the dough in the air, in the air, in the air,
Toss the dough in the air and put it in a pan.

Spread the dough with lots of sauce, lots of sauce,
    lots of sauce,
Spread the dough with lots of sauce, then top it off
    with cheese.

Put some pepperoni on, pepperoni on, pepperoni
    on,
Put some pepperoni on, and don't forget the
    mushrooms.

Bake it in the hot, hot oven, hot, hot oven, hot, hot
    oven,
Bake it in the hot, hot oven, cool it, slice it, eat it!
    YUM!

P-I-Z-Z-A!
(Sing to the tune "BINGO.")

I asked my mother, "What's to eat?"
And this is what she said.
P-I-Z-Z-A
P-I-Z-Z-A
P-I-Z-Z-A
And that is what I had!

I asked my mother, "What's to eat?"
And this is what she said.
"Clap"-I-Z-Z-A
"Clap"-I-Z-Z-A
"Clap"-I-Z-Z-A
And that is what I had!

(Continue until all letters of P-I-Z-Z-A are clapped.)

P Is for Pizza
Finger puppets for this fingerplay can be as simple
as the letters P, I, Z, Z, and A! Find the pattern for
them on the 🔵 CD.

P is for pizza, that's my favorite dish.
A pizza for me; that is my wish!
I is for me, I mean I, that's myself,
I love my pizza; I can't help myself.
Z is for zag and Z is for zig,
The way that my teeth go when my bite is big.
A is for all done, my pizza's all gone.
I baked it and ate it and now there is none!

Vocabulary Builders

New Words and Word Study: Most everyone is familiar with pizza. It's a favorite food!  However, don't assume that children will know the words or terms used in this dramatic play unit. Check for understanding as you use words such as *pizza, pizzeria, toppings, pepperoni, mushrooms, mozzarella, delivery, oven, order, menu, tablecloth,* and *restaurant.*

Onset/Rime: Words that have the same spelling pattern as the word *hot.*

/ot/ cot, dot, hot, pot, tot, spot, trot

Write All About It!

A Week of Pizzas Class Book

Using the days of the week to create the context for a seven-page class book, guide children in writing about their favorite kinds of pizzas. Repeat each day of the week, and the predictable text, *On Monday, (child's name) ate a pizza with _____ on it. On Tuesday (child's name) ate a pizza with _____ on it* and so on. Next, children dictate or write the toppings they've chosen for their favorite pizza. Provide a square sheet of white construction paper as the foundation for each page. Have the children glue a large red circle onto the white paper pizza box, and then add the topping. Toppings can be printed on using tempera paint and appropriate shapes, or drawn using crayons or markers.

Book List

- *Pizza That We Made,* by Joan Holub, Lynne Cravath
- *Curious George and the Pizza*, by Margret Rey
- *Little Red Hen Makes a Pizza*, Retold by Philemon Sturges
- *One Pizza, One Penny*, by K. T. Hao
- *Pete's a Pizza*, by William Steig
- *Veggies on Our Pizza*, by Chantelle B. Goodman, Anthony Morrison
- *Sam's Pizza*, by David Pelham
- *Pizza Party!*, by Grace Maccarone, Emily Arnold McCully
- *Pizza Pat*, by Rita Golden Gelman
- *Pancakes, Crackers, and Pizza: A Book of Shapes*, by Marjorie Eberts, Margaret Gisler
- *Let's Make Pizza*, by Mary Hill
- *Pizza for Sam*, by Mary Labatt, Marisol Sarrazin

Pepperoni, Please! (The End)

Dramatic Creations: Let's Make a Pizza!

Children become the pizza as they take on the roles of the ingredients. Have children sit in a large circle. Outline the inside of the circular shape with a piece of rope or clothesline. Make the circle large enough to have all children sit around.

Have each child select a pizza-ingredient card, which has been prepared in advance. On each card, place the picture and corresponding word or words for a pizza topping. As the ingredients are called out, the children holding those cards enter the circular "pizza," find a position to sit in, and remain there until the pizza is complete.

(The phone rings.)

Pizza Maker: Hello?

Caller: I want to order a pizza.

Pizza Maker: What size do you want?

Caller: I want a very large pizza. I want the largest pizza you can make!

Pizza Maker: What toppings do you want on it?

Caller: I want pepperoni on it.

Pizza Maker: It will have pepperoni on it.

(Children who are holding the pepperoni cards enter the circle and have a seat.)

Caller: I want onions on it.

Pizza Maker: It will have onions on it.

(Children who are holding the onion cards enter the circle and have a seat.)

Caller: I want ham on it.

Pizza maker: It will have ham on it.

(Children who are holding the ham cards enter the circle and have a seat.)

Caller: I want green peppers on it.

Pizza Maker: It will have green peppers on it.

(Children who are holding the green pepper cards enter the circle and have a seat.)

Caller: I want mushrooms on it.

Pizza Maker: It will have mushrooms on it.

(Children who are holding the mushroom cards enter the circle and have a seat.)

Caller: I want pineapple on it.

Pizza Maker: It will have pineapple on it.

(Children who are holding the pineapple cards enter the circle and have a seat.)

Caller: I want one more thing.

Pizza Maker: What is that?

Caller: CHEESE! Lots of cheese!

Pizza Maker: It will have lots of cheese on it.

(Children who are holding the cheese cards enter the circle and have a seat.)

Pizza Maker: Your pizza is ready.

Setting the Stage

Who can resist the sweet smells that float out of a bakery shop? Transform the housekeeping area into a bakery with the help of lots of play dough and plenty of baking tins. For this dramatic theme, involve children as the play dough is made. Write the recipe for play dough on chart paper, so it serves as a constant reference while making the dough. Model the things that recipe readers do while cooking by referring back to the recipe each step along the way.

As a class, brainstorm the various products one might expect in a bakery. Write that list on chart paper and display in the bakery shop. Guide children in referencing the list as they produce different kinds of baked goods. Tint the play dough with food coloring using various colors. This added touch will be enjoyed by both the bakers and customers as they pretend to make and purchase strawberry cakes, blueberry pies, and banana breads.

Once the dough is ready, get out the aprons and chef hats and let the fun begin! Supply the housekeeping area with a variety of baking tins, rolling pins, and cookie cutters. Children bakers will have lots of fun making all kinds of goodies to sell in their bakery. The bakery customers will want to see the sweets displayed. Collect small, clear deli containers (flip-top containers and containers with removable lids) to package the bakery products for sale. Place the items for the customers to see. Doilies under the baked goods add a nice touch. Laminate them for durability and so the play dough won't stick to them.

Turn the puppet theater into the bakery shop check-out counter. Make available a cash register and play money. Shoppers use play grocery carts or baskets to gather up the goodies before they take them to the cashier. Once at the check-out counter, the cashier puts the purchases in bags for the shoppers to take home and enjoy.

Bakeries often provide tables and chairs for their customers. Use placemats on child-sized tables, along with plastic plates for the customers to enjoy their treats, perhaps with a cup of coffee! Set out pretend coffee pots and cups to add to the feeling of a bakery coffee shop. To really set the mood, plug in a cinnamon air freshener into a nearby outlet. The scent will remind the players of cinnamon buns baking in the oven!

Props and Supplies

play dough, food coloring, aprons, chef hats, baking tins of various sizes and shapes (small cake tins, cupcake tins, pie plates, bread pans, cookie sheets), rolling pins, pancake turners, cookie cutters, chart paper, clear deli containers, table or small bookcase, laminated doilies, free standing puppet theater, cash register, play money, child-size grocery carts or baskets, placemats, plastic plates, coffee mugs, coffee pots, and cinnamon air freshener

• What kinds of breads are you baking today?
• How do you think you should package all of these treats?
• How will your customers know what kind of baked goods they can purchase?
• I wonder what kinds of cookies your friends like the best. Do you think you'll be baking any of those today?

Literacy Connections

Songs and Fingerplays

Donuts Everywhere

Donuts, donuts everywhere!
Which one shall I pick?
Chocolate, sprinkles, sugar too,
Icing spread so thick!

I'll pick a donut for my mom,
And daddy gets one too.
I'll pick one for my little sis,
And here's one just for you!

Five Little Cakes

Children will make five little cake finger puppets for this fingerplay using the pattern on the **CD**.

Five little cakes in the bakery store.
The first one said, "I've got flowers galore."
The second one said, "I've got pudding inside."
The third one said, "I've got sprinkles on the side."
The fourth one said, "I've got walnuts in me."
The fifth one said, "I've got layers, one, two, three."
Along came *(child's name)* with four little friends,
And the five little cakes went home with them.

I Wish I Had a Donut

(Sing to the tune "Have You Ever Seen a Lassie?")

I wish I had a donut, a donut, a donut.
I wish I had a donut to gobble up right now.
I'd sniff it and taste it and nibble it and eat it.
I wish I had a donut to gobble up right now.

Other verses:

I wish I had a cookie.
I wish I had a cupcake.
I wish I had a bagel.

Vocabulary Builders

New Words and Word Study: Many children are probably familiar with the grocery store as the place to purchase food of any type. A specialty  store, such as a bakery, offers the opportunity to focus in on terms particular to the items made and sold there. Use terms such as *bakery, baked goods, flour, pie crust, cake batter, cookie dough, biscuits, tarts, donuts, dough, baking tins, baking pans, cookie sheets, rolling pins, purchase, display,* and *placemats.*

Onset/Rime: Words that have the same spelling pattern as the words *bake* and *cake*.

/ake/ bake, cake, lake, rake, take, snake, make, fake, wake, stake, shake

Write All About It!

The Runaway Cookie Class Book

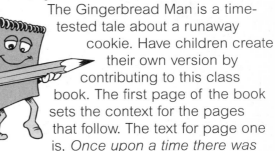

The Gingerbread Man is a time-tested tale about a runaway cookie. Have children create their own version by contributing to this class book. The first page of the book sets the context for the pages that follow. The text for page one is, *Once upon a time there was a baker who loved baking cookies. One day the baker opened the oven and the cookies jumped off of the hot cookie sheet and ran away.* Use the same repetitive text for each subsequent page, *One cookie ran _____.* Have children dictate or write and illustrate where their cookie went.

Book List

- *Walter the Baker*, by Eric Carle
- *At the Bakery*, by Carol Greene
- *Jalapeno Bagels*, by Natasha Wing
- *Bakers*, by Tami Deedrick
- *Arnie, the Doughnut*, by Laurie Keller
- *Cookie Count: A Tasty Pop-Up*, by Robert Sabuda
- *If You Give a Mouse a Cookie*, by Laura Joffe Numeroff
- *Mmmm, Cookies!*, by Robert N. Munsch, Michael Martchenko
- *The Doorbell Rang*, by Pat Hutchins
- *Everybody Bakes Bread*, by Norah Dooley, Peter J. Thornton
- *More Pies!*, by Robert Munsch, Robert N. Munsch
- *I Know an Old Lady Who Swallowed a Pie*, by Alison Jackson, Judith Byron Schachner
- *Thunder Cake*, by Patricia Polacco
- *If You Give a Moose a Muffin*, by Laura Joffe Numeroff, Felicia Bond
- *Who Needs Donuts?*, by Mark Alan Stamaty
- *Gingerbread Man*, by Karen Schmidt

Dramatic Creations: Doughnut Time!

It's time to buy some doughnuts! For this drama have children will make a stop at the bakery to purchase doughnuts. When they enter the bakery, choose a baker to greet them who has several varieties of doughnuts on a tray. Each doughnut is a different kind with different frosting or toppings. Have children create the doughnuts out of paper, but only a few are used at one time.

Each time the shopper says, "I'd like a doughnut please." The baker has to describe the doughnuts. Keep the frosting and other toppings simple and easy to describe such as, "I have a doughnut with white frosting" or "I have a doughnut with nuts on top." There is one baker and there are several shoppers. The number of shoppers is determined by the number of donuts for sale minus one. The last customer does not get a doughnut. He or she will have to come back tomorrow.

Baker: What would you like?

Shopper #1: I'd like a doughnut, please.

Baker: I have a doughnut with …*(for example: …chocolate frosting. I have a doughnut with sprinkles. I have a doughnut with white frosting. I have a doughnut with nuts. I have a doughnut with powdered sugar.)* Which one would you like?

Shopper #1: I'll take that one! *(Shopper takes one of the doughnuts off of the tray. A second customer comes into the bakery.)*

Baker: What would you like?

Shopper #2: I'd like a doughnut, please.

Baker: *(The baker eliminates the doughnut selected by the first customer and describes the remaining doughnuts.)* Which one would you like?

Shopper #2: I'll take that one! *(Shopper takes one of the doughnuts off of the tray. The next shopper comes into the bakery.)*

Baker: What would you like?

Shopper #3: I'd like a doughnut, please.

Baker: *(There are now two doughnuts missing from the tray. The baker names the remaining doughnuts.)* Which one would you like?

Shopper #3: I'll take that one! *(Shopper takes one of the donuts off of the tray. The play continues until all of the doughnuts are gone. The last shopper enters the bakery.)*

Baker: What would you like?

Last Shopper: I'd like a doughnut, please.

Baker: I'm sorry. They're all gone. Please come back tomorrow.

The Grocery Store

Props and Supplies

clean empty plastic or paper food containers, clear packing tape, newspaper, zipper baggies of sand, free standing shelves, classroom tables, cardboard boxes of varying sizes, play shopping carts, shopping baskets, purses, wallets, play money, cash register, grocery bags, coupons, old grocery store tape receipts (laminated), and grocery store uniform (such as matching vests or aprons)

Setting the Stage

Often times the most fun young children have is when enacting everyday events. As families prepare for large family gatherings and bountiful meals that are typical in the late autumn months, children can do so, too, by using familiar props added to the housekeeping area. In preparation, plan a trip to the grocery store. Guide children in using what they learn to create their own store.

Begin by collecting a large quantity and variety of food containers. To ensure the children's safety, use rigid, formed plastic or paper food containers only. Opened metal cans may have sharp edges. Weigh down empty food boxes with a small zipper baggie of sand placed in the bottom of the box. Stuff the remainder of the box with newspaper so that the baggie remains on the bottom. Tape cardboard food boxes shut. Plastic containers with unattached screw on lids will help support the development of fine motor skills as children take the lids on and off.

Find a corner of the classroom away from the housekeeping area where children can use empty book shelves and/or small classroom tables to display the groceries. Cardboard boxes of varying sizes can be used for shelving and for bins of fruits and vegetables. Have children put the merchandise on display. Guide children in creating signs to indicate food groups, such as cereal or pasta.

Young shoppers enter the store and find their shopping cart or basket. They browse up and down the grocery store aisles, selecting items for purchase, then head to the check-out counter where the cashier greets them with a friendly smile. As the customer places the items on the check-out counter, the cashier passes each item over the "scanner" made of a piece of black construction paper taped to the table. The items are moved down the counter to the bagger, who asks the now famous question, "Paper or plastic?"

Have food coupons ready for the customers to use as they pay for their items with play money. The cashier hands the customer their receipt, and then the bagger helps the customer out to their vehicle. Use wagons to transport the purchased groceries home, where they are then placed in the cupboards and refrigerator in the housekeeping area.

- How will you decide to group and display the items on the shelves?
- Are there any foods that need to be kept cold? Where will you keep those?
- Did you find the items that you had coupons for?
- What else might your grocery store sell?

Literacy Connections

Songs and Fingerplays

I've Been Shopping
(Sing to the tune "I've Been Working on the Railroad.")

I've been shopping at the grocery,
To buy the food I need.
I've been shopping at the grocery.
I've got a family to feed.
I've been buying lots of apples,
Some meat and potatoes and peas.
I've been buying lots of corn flakes,
Some eggs and milk and cheese.
Shopping at the store, shopping at the store,
I've been shopping at the store, store, store.
Shopping at the store, shopping at the store,
I've been shopping at the store, store, store.

Grocery Shopping
(Sing to the tune "The Mulberry Bush.")

I'm driving to the grocery store, grocery store,
grocery store.
I'm driving to the grocery store on a Monday
morning.

I'm pushing around the grocery cart, grocery cart,
grocery cart.
I'm pushing around the grocery cart, on a Tuesday
morning.

I'm buying lots of bread and milk, bread and milk,
bread and milk.
I'm buying lots of bread and milk, on a Wednesday
morning.

I'm giving my money to the clerk, to the clerk, to the clerk,
I'm giving my money to the clerk, on a Thursday morning.

I'm loading my groceries in the car, in the car, in the car,
I'm loading my groceries in the car, on a Friday morning.

I'm putting the groceries on the shelf, on the shelf, on the shelf,
I'm putting the groceries on the shelf, on a Saturday morning.

I'm cooking up a great big breakfast, great big breakfast, great big breakfast,
I'm cooking up a great big breakfast, on a Sunday morning.

An additional song can be found on the CD.

Vocabulary Builders

New Words and Word Study: Many children are familiar with grocery shopping. Some words or terms might be unfamiliar to them such as *display case, cooler, produce, freezer, aisle, carts, coupons, clerk, bagger, market, super market, groceries,* and *cupboard.*

Onset/Rime: Words that have the same spelling pattern as the word *bag.*

/ag/ bag, rag, sag, tag, wag, flag, lag

Write All About It!

My Grocery List

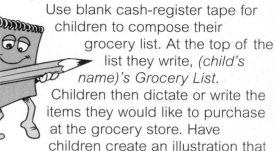

Use blank cash-register tape for children to compose their grocery list. At the top of the list they write, *(child's name)'s Grocery List.* Children then dictate or write the items they would like to purchase at the grocery store. Have children create an illustration that matches each list item. The illustration will serve to support beginning reading skills. Display the grocery lists in the housekeeping area for other children to read.

Book List

- *Don't Forget the Bacon!*, by Pat Hutchins
- *Just Enough Carrots*, by Stuart J. Murphy
- *A Visit to the Supermarket*, by B. A. Hoena
- *Grandpa's Corner Store*, by DyAnne DiSalvo-Ryan
- *Market!*, by Ted Lewin
- *Farmers Market*, by Carmen Parks, Edward Martinez
- *To Market, To Market*, by Anne Miranda
- *On Market Street*, by Arnold Lobel
- *How Are You Peeling? Foods with Moods*, by Saxton Freymann, Joost Elffers
- *I Shop with My Daddy*, by Grace Maccarone, Denise Brunkus
- *Something Good*, by Robert N. Munsch, Michael Martchenko
- *Molly Goes Shopping*, by Eva Eriksson, Elisabeth Kallick Dyssegaard
- *Signs at the Store*, by Mary Hill

The Grocery Store (The End)

Dramatic Creations: Yes, We Have No Bananas!

In this drama, six shoppers each take their turn shopping at the grocery store. They all want the same thing, bananas! Unfortunately, there are none in the store. When the grocer tells them that he has no more bananas, each shopper then tells the grocer that he or she will return on another day.

Shopper #1: Do you have any bananas, please?
Grocer: No, I don't. Would you like some apples?
Shopper #1: No thank you, I'll come back on Monday. *(Shopper leaves the store.)*

Shopper #2: Do you have any bananas, please?
Grocer: No, I don't. Would you like some peaches?
Shopper #2: No thank you, I'll come back on Tuesday. *(Shopper leaves the store.)*

Shopper #3: Do you have any bananas, please?
Grocer: No, I don't. Would you like some watermelon?
Shopper #3: No thank you, I'll come back on Wednesday. *(Shopper leaves the store.)*

Shopper #4: Do you have any bananas, please?
Grocer: No, I don't. Would you like some oranges?
Shopper #4: No thank you, I'll come back on Thursday. *(Shopper leaves the store.)*

Shopper #5: Do you have any bananas, please?
Grocer: No, I don't. Would you like some grapes?
Shopper #5: No thank you, I'll come back on Friday. *(Shopper leaves the store.)*

Shopper #6: Do you have any bananas, please?
Grocer: No, I don't. Would you like some pineapple?
Shopper #6: No thank you, I'll come back on Saturday. *(Shopper leaves the store.)*

Narrator: The next week came and so did the bananas!

Shopper #1: Do you have any bananas, please?
Grocer: Yes, I do! Here they are!
Shopper #1: Thank you very much. *(Shopper leaves the store.)*

Shopper #2: Do you have any bananas, please?
Grocer: Yes, I do! Here they are!
Shopper #2: Thank you very much. *(Shopper leaves the store.)*

Shopper #3: Do you have any bananas, please?
Grocer: Yes, I do! Here they are!
Shopper #3: Thank you very much. *(Shopper leaves the store.)*

Shopper #4: Do you have any bananas, please?
Grocer: Yes, I do! Here they are!
Shopper #4: Thank you very much. *(Shopper leaves the store.)*

Shopper #5: Do you have any bananas, please?
Grocer: Yes, I do! Here they are!
Shopper #5: Thank you very much. *(Shopper leaves the store.)*

Shopper #6: Do you have any bananas, please?
Grocer: Yes, I do! Here they are!
Shopper #6: Thank you very much. *(Shopper leaves the store.)*

Narrator: On Sunday, all of the shoppers had a big feast. They ate banana bread, banana muffins, banana salad, banana pudding, banana cake, and banana cream pie!

Published by Totline Publications. Copyright protected.
1-57029-533-6 *Year 'Round Dramatic Play*

More Autumn Fun

Autumn Art Activities

Autumn Trees: Ask children to create their own autumn tree by using brown crayons to color a tree trunk and branches on a large piece of light blue construction paper. Guide them in adding autumn colored leaves by tearing small pieces of red, yellow, orange, brown, and green construction paper. With a small dot of glue, have them apply the leaves to the branches of the tree as well as the surrounding ground. Perhaps they will glue on some falling leaves, too!

Autumn Tree for the Classroom: Create a 6' autumn tree for the classroom by following the directions in "The Falling Leaves" unit.

Autumn Leaf Collage: Ask children to collect colorful autumn leaves. Dry and press the leaves between sheets of paper toweling, weighted by a flat, heavy object such as a board or a stack of books. Once the leaves are pressed and dry, have the children arrange them on a sheet of clear sticky paper. If there are no deciduous trees in your area, use tissue-paper leaves for this project. Place a second sheet of clear sticky paper over the collage and press until it is sealed. Trim the edges and display in the windows of the classroom.

Pumpkin Prints: Are you carving jack-o-lanterns in your classroom? Save the cut pumpkin pieces to print with in the art center. Cut left-over pumpkin pieces into familiar shapes such as squares, triangles, and circles. Have the children print with the pumpkin pieces by dipping into paint and then stamping onto construction paper.

Autumn Wreath: Have children create autumnal decorations by gluing woodsy autumn finds onto a wreath-shaped piece of cardboard. Go for a nature walk so children can collect autumnal items, such as leaves, nutshells, grasses, or other fall foliage. (As an alternative, provide children with interesting papers such as wall paper, wrapping paper, tissue paper, and craft paper.) Add craft feathers and raffia bows. Glue the items onto the cardboard wreath, overlapping them to fill in empty spaces. Let dry and hang on the wall.

Stencil Leaves: Using a die-cut paper cutter, punch leaf shapes out of laminated construction paper. Use the negative portion, the empty leaf space, for a painting experience in the art center. Lay the laminated stencil onto a large sheet of construction paper and use a sponge painting technique for filling in the shape of the leaf. Carefully lift the stencil and the shape of the leaf will be painted onto the paper. Help children by using color coordinated paper and paint. The red paint will be used with the red stencil, the yellow paint with the yellow stencil, and so on.

More Autumn Fun

Book List for Autumn

- *Fall Is Here! I Love It!*, by Elaine W. Good, Susie Shenk Wenger
- *Fall*, by Patricia Whitehouse
- *It's Fall*, by Jimmy Pickering
- *Autumn Story*, by Jill Barklem
- *Possum's Harvest Moon*, by Anne Hunter
- *Fall*, by Ron Hirschi, Thomas Mangelsen
- *Now It's Fall*, by Lois Lenski
- *It's Fall*, by Linda Glaser
- *Autumn*, by Gail Saunders-Smith
- *Autumn Days*, by Ann Schweninger
- *Animals in the Fall*, by Gail Saunders-Smith
- *Autumn*, by Terri Degezelle
- *I Know It's Autumn*, by Eileen Spinelli

Flannel Board Props

Create felt pieces for the children to use on a flannel board while exploring the following dramatic play themes.

Down on the Farm: barn, farm animals, fencing, milking bucket and stool, farmer, silo, hay bails, hay wagon, eggs, egg baskets, and harvested vegetables

Two fingerplays in this section require chickens: "Ten Little Hens" and "Five Little Chickens Sitting in Their Nest." Provide enough felt chickens for the children to use as props at the flannel board.

An Apple a Day: Apple tree, apples of various sizes and colors, bushel baskets, people, ladders, cider jugs, hay wagon, and a large pie crust with apple slices for filling

Provide at least ten apples to use with the fingerplays in this section.

The Falling Leaves: leaf shapes in various sizes and colors, tree silhouette, rakes, people, wheelbarrows, and clouds "blowing the wind"

"Where Is Red Leaf?" in the songs and fingerplay section requires leaves of various colors. Provide those so children have them as props while singing.

Pumpkin Patch: pumpkins of various shapes and sizes, jack-o-lantern facial features, green stems, vines, candles, hay wagon, bails of hay, and people

The Costume Ball: people with a wide variety of costumes, reminiscent of "paper doll" from the past, horses, a coach, and invitations

Pepperoni, Please!: pizza crust, pizza sauce made from red felt, mushrooms, snips of cream colored yarn for the cheese, green pepper slices, pepperoni circles, pineapple wedges, and onions

Have the letters P, I, Z, Z, and A available for children to sing the "P-I-Z-Z-A!" song.

The Bakery Shop: cake shapes, muffins, doughnuts, cookies, pies, bread, frosting flowers, ovens, bakers with aprons, gingerbread cookies, and a display shelf

"Five Little Cakes" fingerplay requires five uniquely-decorated bakery cakes.

The Grocery Store: a wide variety of food products, shopping bags, shopping cart, and people

Each of the songs and fingerplays in this section mentions specific food. Keep that in mind when making the felt food for this flannel board experience.

1-57029-533-6 *Year 'Round Dramatic Play*

The Toy Store

Props and Supplies

childhood building materials, small boxes of various sizes, craft sticks, pipe cleaners, buttons, fabric and felt scraps, socks, polyester pillow batting, wrapping paper, construction paper, sanded pieces of wood, metal nuts and washers, wooden pegs, other safe hardware items, glue, child-sized tables and/or bookcases, free standing puppet theater, purses, wallets, play money, cash register, bags, and boxes

Setting the Stage

The toys most children play with today are those that have been purchased at a store. Long ago, toys were commonly handmade. They were simpler and called for children to use their imaginations. In this unit, have children make toys and other items to sell in their own toy store.

Provide children with common, childhood building materials, such as Legos®, Tinker Toys®, and Lincoln Logs®. In addition to those, add some small, everyday items like plastic containers, little boxes, craft sticks, pipe cleaners, buttons, socks, construction paper, and wrapping paper. Other items to consider are small wood scraps, which have been sanded to reduce the risk of splinters, metal nuts and washers, wooden pegs, and other safe workshop hardware. Socks can be turned into puppets, or they can be stuffed with polyester pillow batting for dolls. Paper dolls were popular long ago. Teach children how to fold paper and cut out a simple doll shape to make paper dolls.

As a class, brainstorm toys to make. Encourage children to think about their own play, what toys they like to play with, and how they play with those toys. Ask each child to create a picture of a toy they would like to build. Use store catalogs or newspaper inserts from toy stores to use as a reference in helping children think of ways to use the materials provided. Think about and list the materials they will need in the creation process, and discuss how those items can be put together to create toys.

Once the toys have been constructed, set up a corner of the classroom as the toy store. Display the toys on small tables or child-sized book shelves. Label what each toy is and what it might do. Some toys come with a set of instructions on how to put it together. Write simple directions for those that might require some assembly.

Now that the store is ready, invite shoppers. Use a free standing puppet theater for a check-out counter. Provide shoppers with purses or wallets for their play money. Have the cashier use a cash register to keep the money and to make change. Tell customers to carry their purchases in bags or boxes as they leave the toy store.

1-57029-533-6 *Year 'Round Dramatic Play*

Literacy Connections

Songs and Fingerplays

I Went to the Toy Store Today
(Sing to the tune "Animal Fair.")

I went to the toy store today,
To buy some blocks to play.
I'll build a house,
Just right for a mouse,
That's what I want to play.

I went to the toy store today,
To buy a doll to play.
I'll sing her a song,
All the day long,
That's what I want to play.

I went to the toy store today,
To buy a train to play.
Go round the track,
On it's way back,
That's what I want to play.

I went to the toy store today,
To buy a ball to play.
I'll bounce it high,
Up to the sky,
That's what I want to play.

The Toy That I Imagine

The toy that I imagine,
Is one that moves around.
It whirls and spins and does a flip,
In the air or on the ground.

The toy that I imagine,
Is one that makes me laugh.
It makes a lot of bubbles,
With me in the bath.

The toy that I imagine,
Is one that shines so bright.
Colors of the rainbow,
Dancing in the night.

The toy that I imagine,
Is one that I can hold.
To keep me warm and snuggly,
Against the winter's cold.

I'm a Little Toy
(Sing to the tune "I'm a Little Teapot.")

Sing each verse using a different color. Have children wearing the corresponding color enter the circle and do the motions in the song. Put color words on cards and select one for each verse of the song.

I'm a little blue toy.
Watch me spin.
I jump and run,
And spin again.
When I get all tired I sit right down,
On the safe and steady ground.

Other verses:
I'm a little red toy....
I'm a little yellow toy....
And so on.

Vocabulary Builders

New Words and Word Study: Toys are the tools for young children! They are probably  very familiar with the names of the toys, especially those that are connected to television. In this section, focus on new words relevant to the toys they're building. Also focus on structural and functional words that describe the parts of the toys as well as what the toy does. Other words to use: *assemble, construct, build, display, purchase,* and *package.*

Onset/Rime: Words that have the same spelling pattern as the word *zip.*

/ip/ *dip, hip, lip, sip, tip, zip, ship, chip, drip, trip*

Write All About It!

Toy Store Catalog Class Book

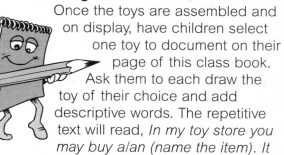 Once the toys are assembled and on display, have children select one toy to document on their page of this class book. Ask them to each draw the toy of their choice and add descriptive words. The repetitive text will read, *In my toy store you may buy a/an (name the item). It is very (describing word or words).* For example, the text might read, *In my toy store you may buy a car. It is very fast.* Bind the pages together and make a catalog for the classroom library.

BOOK List

- *Corduroy*, by Don Freeman
- *Curious George Visits a Toy Store*, by Martha Weston
- *The Little Engine That Could*, by Watty Piper
- *William's Doll*, by Charlotte Zolotow
- *The Toy Shoppe*, by Kenny Rogers, Kelly Junkermann
- *Alexander and the Wind-Up Mouse*, by Leo Lionni
- *Angelina and the Rag Doll*, by Katharine Holabird
- *Apple Doll*, by Kathleen Phillips Poulse
- *Where's My Teddy?*, by Jez Alborough
- *Worry Bear*, by Charlotte Dematons
- *Architect of the Moon*, by Tim Wynne-Jones
- *Pocket for Corduroy*, by Don Freeman
- *Babushka's Doll*, by Patricia Polacco

Dramatic Creations: The Toy Store

Children will have fun pretending to be toys in this guided drama! Select six children to be customers who come to a toy store to purchase specific toys. The remaining children act out the actions of each toy requested as the narrator describes those actions to the customer.

Narrator: Good morning! May I help you?

Customer #1: Yes, I would like a toy, please.

Narrator: Which one would you like?

Customer #1: I would like some blocks.

Narrator: We have blocks. You can line them up. *(Children who are sitting in the circle will get on their hands and knees.)* They might all topple down. *(Children will drop to the ground, and then return to a seated position for the next action.)*

Customer #1: Thank you.

(Customer #1 exits. Customer #2 enters.)

Narrator: Good morning! May I help you?

Customer #2: Yes, I would like a toy, please.

Narrator: Which one would you like?

Customer #2: I would like a car.

Narrator: We have cars. *(Children get on their hands and knees and are ready to move about as cars once given the signal.)* They can move fast, *(Children move about on their hands and knees quickly.)* and they can move slow. *(Children move slowly, then return to their seats in the circle.)*

Customer #2: Thank you.

(Customer #2 exits. Customer #3 enters.)

Narrator: Good morning! May I help you?

Customer #3: Yes, I would like a toy, please.

Narrator: Which one would you like?

Customer #3: I would like a train.

Narrator: We have trains. *(Children stand in a circle and place their hands on the shoulders of the children in front of them.)* We have trains that move on tracks. *(Children begin to move in a circle.)* We have trains that have whistles. *(Children say, "Toot, Toot!")*

Customer #3: Thank you.

(Customer #3 exits. Customer #4 enters.)

Narrator: Good morning! May I help you?

Customer #4: Yes, I would like a toy, please.

Narrator: Which one would you like?

Customer #4: I would like a ball.

Narrator: We have balls. *(Children bring their knees up to the chests, round like a ball.)* These balls roll and roll and roll and roll. *(Children roll about on the floor and then return to their seats.)*

Customer #4: Thank you.

(Customer #4 exits. Customer #5 enters.)

Narrator: Good morning! May I help you?

Customer #5: Yes, I would like a toy, please.

Narrator: Which one would you like?

Customer #5: I would like a horse.

Narrator: We have horses. We have horses that gallop, *(Children gallop around in a circle.)* and horses that neigh. *(Children "neigh," then return to their seats.)*

Customer #5: Thank you.

(Customer #5 exits. Customer #6 enters.)

Narrator: Good morning! May I help you?

Customer #6: Yes, I would like a toy, please.

Narrator: Which one would you like?

Customer #6: I would like a doll.

Narrator: We have dolls. Dolls that hug, *(Children give themselves a big hug.)* dolls that cry, *(Children begin to cry and rub their eyes.)* and dolls that sleep. *(Children cuddle up on the floor and pretend to sleep.)*

Customer #6: Thank you.

(Customer #6 exits.)

Wrap It Up!

Props and Supplies

tempera paint, paintbrushes, low tables, bookshelves, gift boxes, wrapping paper, bows, tape, safety scissors, holiday decorations, eight-inch Styrofoam rounds, Styrofoam balls, wooden pegs, party hats, craft items (such as yarn, beads, wooden craft sticks), glue, clay, play dough, tissue paper, construction paper, pipe cleaners, plastic containers, art foam, fabric scraps, buttons, and felt pieces

Setting the Stage

Gift giving is a year-round occurrence. There are birthdays, weddings, holidays, and other gifts just for fun. During the holiday season, however, it's traditional in many cultures to give a little gift. Carry over this idea and give children the opportunity to "shop" in their own gift shop and have their gift wrapped as well! Use holiday catalogs to prompt children to think about what kinds of gifts they would like to have in their gift shop. Brainstorm and write ideas on chart paper. Encourage children to think about items that can be made such as their own art work, bracelets made from yarn and beads, wooden craft-stick sculptures or photo frames, clay or play dough crafts, flowers made from tissue paper and pipe cleaners, vases made from plastic containers or frozen juice containers, and so on. As the items are completed, display in a section of the classroom set aside for the gifts. Use low tables or bookshelves to hold the items for sale. Customers shop for their "gifts," and then take their purchases to the gift wrap counter.

Designate a separate table for wrapping. Provide small boxes for the gifts, as well as a supply of wrapping paper and bows. Use a variety of wrapping paper so children may give a gift for different occasions. Precut the wrapping paper into appropriate sizes, or allow the children to use safety scissors as they cut a piece of wrapping paper that is just the right size. Support children in this by demonstrating how they can judge the amount of paper needed to wrap a gift and then how to wrap a gift. Have children take their purchases to the check-out counter and pay using play money. Provide a cash register.

Once the gifts are made, purchased, and wrapped, have children give gifts in a variety of ways. Supply birthday party props so children can celebrate someone's special day. Guide children in transforming eight-inch Styrofoam rounds into birthday cakes. Ice cream is served in the form of Styrofoam balls. Provide colorful wooden pegs for birthday candles. Everyone wears a party hat! The "birthday" child will open their gifts once the candles are blown out. Children may also pretend it's a specific holiday such as Christmas, Hanukkah, or Valentine's Day. Let the play unfold as the children act out their family traditions. Return the opened gifts to the gift shop where they may be purchased and wrapped again and again until the gift shop closes. Children who have made something for the gift shop will want their item once the play is over. Make sure to label each creation with the children's name and see that the items are returned to their owner.

• What kinds of things have you seen for sale at the store that would make a great gift?
• Where will we get these items?
• Are there any that we can make ourselves?
• How will you know how much wrapping paper you will need to wrap each present?
• I wonder how you can tell what's inside of a wrapped package before you open it.

Literacy Connections

Songs and Fingerplays

Presents

A present for you and a present for me,
Wrapped up so pretty under the tree!
I wonder what's in there, what could it hold?
Is it a sweater, a book, or some gold?

A present for you and a present for me,
Wrapped up so pretty under the tree!
I'll open it now, and then I will see.
The wonderful present that was given to me.

I Have a G-I-F-T, Gift

I have a g-i-f-t gift,
That I wrapped up for y-o-u.
And I m-a-d-e, made it using,
Lots of stuff and glue.

It isn't h-a-r-d, hard,
To think what it could b-e, be.
It's a _____.*
A little gift to you from me!

*(*Prepare "gift" cards to use when you come to this part of the song/poem. Have children say the individual letters and then the word, as patterned in the song.)*

I'm Bringing Home a Gift

(Sing to the tune "I'm Bringing Home a Baby Bumble Bee.")

I'm bringing home a little gift or two.
It will be a big surprise for you.
A bright blue- and red-striped racing car,
Wind it up and let it go far.

I'm bringing home a little gift or two.
It will be a big surprise for you.
A warm and fuzzy friendly teddy bear,
Give him a hug and put him in a chair.

I'm bringing home a little gift or two.
It will be a big surprise for you.
A bouncing ball that bounces way up high,
Bouncing right up to the sky.

Literacy Connections (cont.)

Vocabulary Builders

New Words and Word Study: There are many occasions to give and receive gifts. Emphasize common terms such as *present, gift, gift wrap, ribbon, bows, package, receive, give, send, surprise, holiday,* and *occasion.*

Onset/Rime: Words that have the same spelling pattern as the word *gift.*

/ift/ gift, lift, sift, drift, shift, swift

Write All About It!

Give a Gift Class Book

Gifts are not always about giving a present. They are often about giving of ourselves.

Encourage children to think about ways to give a gift of time or love to their family or friends such as sweeping the floor, picking up their toys, giving a hug. For this class book, have each child write and illustrate about a gift of time or love to give. The text for this will vary depending on what act of kindness is given. Keep the text simple so young readers are supported in their rereading of this book. For example the text might read, *I will rake the lawn for Grandpa.* Or, *Carolyn washed the dishes for her family.*

Book List

- *The Giving Tree*, by Shel Silverstein
- *Something Special for Me*, by Vera B. Williams
- *Yoko's Paper Cranes*, by Rosemary Wells
- *A Mud Pie for Mother*, by Scott Beck
- *Manuela's Gift*, by Kristyn Estes, Claire Cotts
- *The Giving Bear (Winnie the Pooh First Reader)*, by Isabel Gaines
- *Emeka's Gift: An African Counting Story (Picture Puffins)*, by Ifeoma Onyefulu
- *Alejandro's Gift*, by Richard E. Albert
- *Gwendolyn's Gift*, by Patty Sheehan, Claudia Bumgarner-Kirby
- *Sea Gifts*, by George Shannon, Mary Azarian
- *Lion's Precious Gift*, by Barbara Bennett, Amanda Hall

Wrap It Up! (The End)

Dramatic Creations: What Could It Be?

What's inside of that great big box? What's underneath that pretty paper and bow? Have children guess as a child "gift" inside a box pantomimes the actions of some common items. For this drama you will need to find a large cardboard box, one that a child can fit into. Cut off one side of the box and make a door out of the opposite side. Wrap the box in festive paper, leaving the cut side open and the door side functional. Beautiful bows on top will make this box look like a present.

One at a time, have children enter the box through the open end. When they hear the signal, they emerge through the door side of the box and begin to pantomime the actions of the item they're pretending to be. For example, a child pantomiming a car might use their hand to turn the steering wheel and their feet for the gas pedal and brake.

All Children Chant: I wonder what is in the box.

Child #1: *(Emerges through the door of the box and begins to pantomime. Children sitting in the circle begin to guess what gift Child #1 is acting out. When the children correctly guess the pantomime, the performing child returns to the circle and the play continues.)*

All Children Chant: I wonder what is in the box.

Child #2: *(Emerges through the door of the box and begins to pantomime. Children sitting in the circle begin to guess what gift Child #2 is acting out. When the children correctly guess the pantomime, the performing child returns to the circle and the play continues.)*

Suggested gifts include those things which are tangible such as a bike, a top, a ball, a clock, as well as gifts of time and love such as sweeping the floor, washing the dishes, making the bed, and setting the table.

 1-57029-533-6 *Year 'Round Dramatic Play*

Trim a Tree

Props and Supplies

artificial pine trees with stands, polyester quilt batting, holiday tree lights, packing peanuts, large plastic sewing needles, yarn, tape, beads, pinecones, peanut butter, bird seed, yarn, battery-operated candles, holiday-specific candle holders, small boxes, gift wrap, bows, artificial pine boughs, and tree ornaments

Setting the Stage

Winter is a traditional time for family gatherings, holiday celebrations, and fanciful decorations to adorn homes, neighborhoods, and stores. Allow children the opportunity to "dress up" their classroom in a similar fashion. There's no need to focus on specific holidays. For the children, this is a time to transform their classroom into a sparkling, light-filled display of holiday trimmings. Provide children with all the trimmings they need to transform a corner of the classroom into a winter wonderland. Artificial pine trees in varying sizes will create the winter backdrop. Add twinkle lights to the trees. Use white to resemble sparkling snow or colorful lights common at holiday time.

Trim trees for winter by using shapes of polyester batting used for quilts. Cut shapes of batting to drape over the branches to resemble freshly fallen snow and cut snowflakes. Use full sheets of batting to tuck in around the base of the trees. Drape handmade garlands from the snow-laden branches. Have children use packing peanuts and plastic needles threaded with yarn to string. Make other garlands by using large beads and yarn. To assist children in threading the beads, wrap masking tape around the end of the yarn to provide a sturdy end for poking through the eye of the needle. Tape the other end of the yarn to the table, so all of the children's handiwork doesn't slide off!

Other holiday decorations will be determined by your emphasis. If celebrating a specific holiday, provide children with the props and supplies to do so. Battery-operated candles are safe for children to use and will allow them to enact the ceremonies they may see within their cultures and homes. If using candles or their replicas, emphasize safety with your children. Never play with matches or with lit candles. Little gifts can be wrapped and placed under the tree for an added dimension of realism. Trim trees outside for the birds! Select a tree by a window where children can observe the action. Using pinecones, peanut butter, and bird seed, make individual bird feeders for our feathered friends. Guide children in spreading peanut butter onto pine cones, and then rolling it in bird seed. A little loop of yarn tied onto the pine cone allows the children to place the little feeder onto the tree.

However you choose to decorate the classroom or a nearby tree outdoors, include the children in the preparations and allow them the flexibility to arrange and rearrange ornaments, garlands, and other trims and props.

• What things will you use to decorate your tree?
• I wonder why so many people decorate with lights.
• Are there any decorations that you can make?
• How would you decorate a tree outdoors?

Literacy Connections

Songs and Fingerplays

Twinkle, Twinkle, Little Lights
(Sing to the tune "Twinkle, Twinkle, Little Star.")

Twinkle, Twinkle, little lights,
Shining brightly through the night.
Twinkling, flickering, dancing so.
Give off such a cozy glow.
Twinkle, Twinkle, little lights,
Shining brightly through the night.

Trim a Tree
(Sing to the tune "Row, Row, Row Your Boat.")

Trim, trim, trim a tree,
Dress it up so bright.
Garlands, baubles, balls, and beads,
Shining in the night.

Five Little Candles
Use the candle pattern on the **CD** to create five candle finger puppets to use while reciting this fingerplay.

Five little candles shining bright,
Lit up the darkness, gave it light.
The wind came along and with a little puff,
(Blow on one candle.)
Made the lights flicker and one said, "Enough!"
(Remove one candle finger puppet.)

Four little candles shining bright,
Lit up the darkness, gave it light.

The wind came along and with a little puff, *(Blow on one candle.)*
Made the lights flicker and one said, "Enough!"
(Remove one candle finger puppet.)

Three little candles shining bright,
Lit up the darkness, gave it light.
The wind came along and with a little puff, *(Blow on one candle.)*
Made the lights flicker and one said, "Enough!"
(Remove one candle finger puppet.)

Two little candles shining bright,
Lit up the darkness, gave it light.
The wind came along and with a little puff, *(Blow on one candle.)*
Made the lights flicker and one said, "Enough!"
(Remove one candle finger puppet.)

One little candle shining bright,
Lit up the darkness, gave it light.
The wind came along and with a little puff, *(Blow on the last candle.)*
Made the light flicker and the last one said, "Enough!" *(Remove last candle finger puppet.)*

Vocabulary Builders

New Words and Word Study: The words you
focus on will depend on the direction
taken with this section. Common
words to use are those such as
*celebrations, holiday,
decorations, glittery, shining,
trim, lights, evergreens, holly,* and
boughs.

Onset/Rime: Words that have the same spelling
pattern as the word *trim.*

/im/ dim, him, rim, slim, swim, trim, brim

Write All About It!

My Winter Tree Class Book

Have children use an evergreen
tree template, found on the
accompanying 🆔 , and
decorate it with specific
items, numbered one through
five. The repetitive text will read,
*On (Child's name) tree he/she put,
one (name item), two (name
items), three (name items), four
(name items), five (name items).* For example, a
holiday tree might be decorated with: one star,
two green balls, three lights, four garlands, five
red balls. A seasonal tree dressed for the
outdoors might include: one bird feeder, two
strings of popcorn, three red birds, four
squirrels, five snowflakes. Bind the pages
together as a class book and place in the
classroom book corner.

Book List

- *Lights of Winter: Winter Celebrations Around the World*,
    by Heather Conrad, deForest Walker
- *The Trees of the Dancing Goats*, by Patricia Polacco
- *Night Tree*, by Eve Bunting, Ted Rand
- *The Snow Tree*, by Caroline Repchuk
- *The Beautiful Christmas Tree*, by Charlotte Zolotow
- *Mooseltoe*, by Margie Palatini, Henry Cole
- *Cobweb Christmas: The Tradition of Tinsel*, by Shirley Climo
- *Little Tree*, by E. E. Cummings
- *The Star Tree*, by Gisela Colle, Rosemary Lanning
- *The Most Beautiful Tree*, by Melody Carlson, Donna Race
- *Light the Lights!: A Story About Celebrating Hanukkah and Christmas*,
    by Margaret Moorman
- *Seven Candles for Kwanzaa*, by Andrea Davis Pinkney
- *My First Kwanzaa*, by Karen Katz
- *Redbird at Rockefeller Center*, by Peter Maloney, Felicia Zekauskas

Dramatic Creations:
Trim a Tree...For the Holidays, or ...For the Birds

In each version of this winter drama, have several children dress up as trees while groups of children are called upon to decorate. Create sandwich-board type trees for several children to wear. Measure the heights of your children from their shoulder to their ankles. Cut pieces of cardboard appropriate to that length. Ask children to paint an evergreen tree on the one side of each piece of cardboard. Attach the two pieces of cardboard at the tops using twine. Leave adequate space between the pieces of cardboard to allow children to slip their tree costumes over their heads. Using sticky back Velcro®, place one-inch pieces of the hook-sided Velcro® onto the trees. Have children create paper decorations for the trees. Laminate these and then place the fuzzy side of the Velcro® onto the backs of the decorations. During the drama, ask children to decorate the trees, placing their decoration onto the Velcro®.

The decorations the children make will depend on the type of tree you emphasize in this section. A holiday tree will have brightly colored ornaments of various shapes and sizes, as well as a star for the top of the tree. An outdoor tree will be home to birds, bird feeders, popcorn strings, snowflakes, and icicles.

Narrator: Once there were *(number of trees)* lonely trees. No one had come to see them. No one had decorations for them. Then one day *(corresponding number of children)* children came along and saw the lonely trees. The trees were feeling sad.

Children: We have some decorations for you. Here they are. *(Children place their decorations on the trees, matching the Velcro™ to that of the ornament.)*

Narrator: The lonely trees were feeling happy.

Trees: Thank you.

Children: You're welcome.

Trees: Look at how lovely we look! *(The trees remain standing while the children who decorated them return to their seats.)*

Narrator: Soon more children came along and saw the little trees.

Children: We have some decorations for you. Here they are.

Narrator: The trees were feeling very happy.

Trees: Thank you.

Children: You're welcome.

Trees: Look at how splendid we look! *(Children leave and return to their seats.)*

Narrator: Soon more children came along and saw the little trees.

Children: We have some decorations for you. Here they are.

Narrator: The trees were feeling very, very happy.

Trees: Thank you.

Children: You're welcome.

Trees: Look at how elegant we look! *(Children leave and return to their seats.)*

Narrator: Soon more children came along and saw the little trees.

Children: We have some decorations for you. Here they are.

Narrator: The trees were feeling very, very, very happy.

Trees: Thank you.

Children: You're welcome.

Trees: Look at how magnificent we look! *(Children leave and return to their seats.)*

Narrator: The trees were feeling very, very, very, very happy and not because they looked so lovely or splendid, or elegant, or magnificent. They were very, very, very, very happy because the children made them feel loved.

Where Are the Bears?

Props and Supplies

free standing dome tent, white sheet, grey construction paper, scissors, tape, winter trees (bare branches and/or small artificial evergreen trees), quilting batting, tagboard, sleeping bags, pillows, books, lullaby CD's, flashlights, plastic food, blue tarp or construction paper, paper fish, and play cameras

Setting the Stage

Not all animals love the winter! Some creatures, such as certain birds and butterflies, travel to the south for the winter where the weather is much warmer. Others, like bears, spend their winters sleeping, waiting for the warmer weather of spring to come and find them! Create a bear cave in the classroom for your young children to enjoy on a cold and snowy winter's day.

Transform a free standing, dome tent into a bear cave for your "cubs" to use as they hibernate during the winter. To make the tent look more like a cave in the winter, drape the tent with a plain, white sheet. Children may add paper rocks to the exterior of the cave by cutting grey construction paper and then taping the rocks onto the sheet. If a tent is not available, use adult-sized tables draped with white sheets instead. Make sure to accommodate for a door to the cave!

Construct a forest backdrop using bare tree branches "planted" in large buckets of sand or plaster of Paris and small artificial evergreen trees. Decorate the trees with "snow" made from quilting batting. Have children place artificial winter birds on the trees that you purchased or by creating feathered friends of your own in the art center. Make the paper birds out of tagboard for longer use.

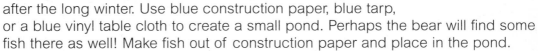

Inside the cave, provide some comforts for the little bears such as sleeping bags and pillows, books about bears, lullaby cd's, and flashlights. Guide children in taking on family roles: papa bear, mama bear, and the baby bears. Papa and Mama Bears may have to cajole their little ones into the long winter nap! When it's time to wake up, the bear family will be hungry. Make sure there are plenty of "treats" for them to eat. Place plastic food items around and near the bear cave so the bears will easily find their food once they've awakened. Create a little pond for the bears as well. They will be thirsty after the long winter. Use blue construction paper, blue tarp, or a blue vinyl table cloth to create a small pond. Perhaps the bear will find some fish there as well! Make fish out of construction paper and place in the pond.

After they've eaten and are full, the bears will surely want to go for a walk. They may see some people along the way who will want to take their photo! Have a play camera ready.

1-57029-533-6 *Year 'Round Dramatic Play*

- How do you think bears know when it's time to hibernate?
- I wonder if bears really do sleep all winter. Do you think that they wake up at all?
- How would you feel if you slept all winter long? What would you miss the most?
- How do you think the bears know when it's time to wake up again?

Literacy Connections

Songs and Fingerplays

Are You Sleepy?
(Sing to the tune "Are you Sleeping, Brother John.")

Have children use the bear family finger puppets for this song from the accompanying CD.

Are you sleepy?
Are you sleepy?
Mr. Bear, Mr. Bear.
Now it's time for sleeping.
Close your eyes, no peeking.
Sleep, sleep, sleep,
In your cave so deep.

Other verses:
Mrs. Bear
Brother Bear
Sister Bear
Baby Bear

Ten Little Bears
(Sing to the tune "Ten Little Indians.")

One little, two little, three little bears,
Four little, five little, six little bears,
Seven little, eight little, nine little bears,
Ten bears ready for sleep.

They crawled in the warm cave and then they yawned.
They crawled in the warm cave and then they yawned.

They crawled in the warm cave and then they yawned.
Ten bears ready for sleep.

They put on pajamas and brushed their teeth.
They put on pajamas and brushed their teeth.
They put on pajamas and brushed their teeth.
Ten bears ready for sleep.

They pulled up the blankets around their shoulders.
They pulled up the blankets around their shoulders.
They pulled up the blankets around their shoulders.
Ten bears ready for sleep.

They said good night, and turned out the lights.
They said good night, and turned out the lights.
They said good night, and turned out the lights.
Ten bears ready for sleep.

One little, two little, three little bears,
Four little, five little, six little bears,
Seven little, eight little, nine little bears,
Ten bears sleeping so deep.

An additional song can be found on the CD.

Literacy Connections (cont.)

Vocabulary Builders

New Words and Word Study: Bears live in many parts of the country; however, it is likely that your children have only seen them in the zoo or in books. Words to focus on in this section are: *hibernation, cave, bears, cubs, season, winter, snowfall,* and *forest.*

Onset/Rime: Words that have the same spelling pattern as the word *cave.*

/ave/ *cave, gave, save, wave, brave, shave*

Write All About It!

Good Night, Bear Class Book

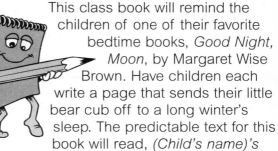 This class book will remind the children of one of their favorite bedtime books, *Good Night, Moon,* by Margaret Wise Brown. Have children each write a page that sends their little bear cub off to a long winter's sleep. The predictable text for this book will read, *(Child's name)'s bear said good night to _____.* Ask children to name the item to be written in the space and illustrate the text accordingly. Bind together as a class book. Illustrate the cover with the entrance to a cave, a much welcome sight to a sleepy bear!

Book List

- *Bear Snores On*, by Karma Wilson
- *A Bed for Winter*, by Karen Wallace
- *Copy Me, Copycub*, by Richard Edwards
- *Snow Bear*, by Miriam Moss, Maggie Kneen
- *The Mitten: A Ukrainian Folktale*, Adapted by Jan Brett
- *How Do Bears Sleep?*, by E. J. Bird
- *Sleepy Bear*, by Lydia Dabcovich
- *Bear on the Train*, by Julie Lawson, Brian Deines
- *Every Autumn Comes the Bear*, by Jim Arnosky
- *Time to Sleep*, by Denise Fleming
- *Bear Wants More*, by Karma Wilson
- *Goodnight Moon*, by Margaret Wise Brown

Where Are the Bears? (The End)

Dramatic Creations: The Just Right Cave

This drama has a bear family looking for the "just right" cave for their hibernation in the winter. They will explore various caves, but each will have their faults until they come upon the cave that is "just right." Cast of characters include Papa Bear, Mama Bear, and Baby Bear. Have children create bear masks using paper plates. Cut holes for the eyes and mouth. Guide children in adding brown bear ears and a dark bear nose. Use string or yarn to tie the mask onto the children actors.

Narrator: On a cold, blustery day the bear family went out looking for a cave in which to take their long winter's nap. They walked up to a cave that seemed just right.

Papa Bear: This cave is too dark.

Mama Bear: This cave is too light.

Baby Bear: I think this cave is just right!

Narrator: The bear family moved on to another cave.

Papa Bear: The ground is too dry.

Mama Bear: The ground is too wet.

Baby Bear: I think the ground is just right!

Narrator: The bear family moved on to another cave.

Papa Bear: The air is too stale.

Mama Bear: The air is too fresh.

Baby Bear: I think the air is just right!

Narrator: The bear family moved on to another cave.

Papa Bear: The walls are too thick.

Mama Bear: The walls are too thin.

Baby Bear: I think the walls are just right!

Narrator: Finally, the bear family came to the last cave in the forest. They all went in.

Papa Bear: The light is just right!

Mama Bear: I agree.

Baby Bear: I agree.

Papa Bear: The ground is just right!

Mama Bear: I agree.

Baby Bear: I agree.

Papa Bear: The air is just right!

Mama Bear: I agree.

Baby Bear: I agree.

Papa Bear: The walls are just right!

Mama Bear: I agree.

Baby Bear: I agree.

Narrator: So the bear family went to the back of the cave, lay down, closed their eyes, and took a long, long winter's nap in their just right cave.

Props and Supplies

large plastic tarp, chairs or benches, large socks, cd player, large cardboard boxes, child-sized brooms, 1/2" dowel, string, magnets, paper fish, paper clips, children's plastic skis, traffic cones, plastic sleds and saucers, clothesline, winter garments (such as scarves, hats, goggles, gloves, boots, bulky sweaters), and quilting batting

Setting the Stage

Figure skating, hockey games, and ice fishing: these are just a few of the fun winter sports that people who live in snow country can enjoy outdoors. Have children experience the fun of playing these icy sports in the classroom. Choose one, two, or all these sports to focus on in this section! Create an indoor skating rink by providing a large blue plastic tarp spread out on the floor in a corner of the classroom. Your ice rink will need nearby benches or chairs for the skaters as they change from their shoes into their "skates," which take the form of large woolly socks. Children will get a little glide on the vinyl tarp by just wearing socks. Play "Skater's Waltz," so children can skate with a partner around their indoor skating rink.

Turn the rink into a hockey rink by adding goals at each end using large cardboard boxes and child-sized brooms for hockey sticks. Roll a sock into a ball to use as a safe puck for the play. Be sure to set some ground rules for this game and supervise closely! Clean up the ice with a cardboard box Zamboni between periods and at the end of the game. When the hockey game is over, keep the tarp out and turn it into a lake for ice-fishing! No need for boats with this kind of sport. Set up a small ice fishing shanty by using a large cardboard box, refrigerator size. Fishing poles for this sport are short. Use 1/2" dowel cut into one-foot lengths. Tie a string around the end of

each pole and attach a magnet to the other end of the string. Have children create fish out of paper, decorating them on both sides. A paper clip at the mouth of the fish allows children to catch them with their fishing poles.

Other winter fun includes skiing, sledding, and dog sledding. Purchase child-sized plastic skis and mark off a course within the classroom. Create a slalom run by using chairs or traffic cones from them to weave their way through. Bring in plastic sleds and saucers for children to pretend that they're sailing downhill in the slippery snow. A large cardboard box and some clothesline are transformed into a dog-sledding team.

The prop box needs some clothes! Add colorful scarves, hats, mittens, ski goggles, boots, and bulky sweaters. Create a backdrop using artificial evergreen trees laden with quilter's batting snow. The stage is now set. Let the winter games begin!

- How do people stay warm out in the snow all day?
- How will you warm up after a day in the snow?
- I wonder why the water in the pond doesn't freeze all the way to the bottom.
- Which winter sport is your favorite?

Literacy Connections

Songs and Fingerplays

I'm Skating
I'm skating; I'm skating on the ice
Around the rink I go.
I'm jumping, I'm twirling, this is so nice.
I'm skating as it snows.

I'm skiing; I'm skiing down the hill
Through the gates I go.
I'm jumping, I'm shushing, this is a thrill.
I'm skiing in the snow.

I'm fishing; I'm fishing through the ice.
I've got a fish on my pole.
I'm pulling; I'm pulling the fish through the ice.
I'm fishing, watch it snow.

I'm sledding; I'm sledding, away I fly
Down the hill I go.
I'm darting and dashing and zooming by.
The sledders on the snow.

This Is the Way I Ski Down the Hill
(Sing to the tune "This Is the Way I Wash My Clothes.")

Children stand during this song and act out each of the events.

This is the way I ski down the hill,
Ski down the hill, ski down the hill.
This is the way I ski down the hill on a winter's
    morning.

This is the way I skate on the ice,
Skate on the ice, skate on the ice.
This is the way I skate on the ice on a winter's
    morning.

This is the way I sled down the hill,
Sled down the hill, sled down the hill.
This is the way I sled down the hill on a winter's
    morning.

This is the way I fish through the ice,
Fish through the ice, fish through the ice.
This is the way I fish through the ice on a winter's
    morning.

Five on a Toboggan Fingerplay
Five on a toboggan, going down the hill,
They hit a bump and took a spill.
One little rider said, "I'm all done!"
So four went back for another run.

Four on a toboggan, going down the hill.
They hit a bump and took a spill.
One little rider said, "I'm all done!"
So three went back for another run.

Three on a toboggan, going down the hill,
They hit a bump and took a spill.
One little rider said, "I'm all done!"
So two went back for another run.

Two on a toboggan, going down the hill,
They hit a bump and took a spill.
One little rider said "I'm all done!"
So one went back for another run.

One on a toboggan, going down the hill,
He hit a bump and took a spill.
The last little rider said, "I'm all done!"
So they all went home after their fun.

Vocabulary Builders

New Words and Word Study: The concept of snow sports might be new to those who live in warmer climates. Words and terms to focus on are: *ice rink, figure skating, twirl, hockey, slippery, skis, skiing, ski lift, shush, dog team, dog sledding, toboggan, slalom, course, ice fishing shanty, ski boots, parka,* and *wintery.*

Onset/Rime: Words that have the same spelling pattern as the word *hill.*

/ill/ bill, fill, hill, pill, chill, spill, mill, will, drill

Write All About It!

My Favorite Sport Class Book

What is your favorite wintertime sport? Give children the opportunity to express that in this class book. They will write or dictate, *(Child's name)'s favorite winter sport is* _____. The accompanying illustration should correspond to their text. Use blue construction paper for their crayon drawings. Add snow by having the children lightly spray white tempera paint onto the drawing by using a small water mister and slightly diluted white tempera paint. Once dry, add the text message.

Book List

- *Curious George in the Snow*, by Margret Rey, H. A. Rey
- *Angelina Ice Skates*, by Katharine Holabird, Helen Craig
- *Slip! Slide! Skate!,* by Gail Herman, Paige Billin-Frye
- *Jack and Jill and Big Dog Bill*, by Martha Weston
- *Dogteam*, by Gary Paulsen
- *First Snow*, by Emily Arnold McCully
- *Meg and Jim's Sled Trip*, by Laura Appleton-Smith
- *Omar on Ice*, by Maryann Kovalski
- *Z Is for Zamboni: A Hockey Alphabet*, by Matt Napier
- *That's Hockey,* by Dean Griffiths, David Bouchard
- *Ollie's Ski Trip*, by Elsa Maartman Beskow, Elsa Beskow
- *A Perfect Day for It*, by Jan Fearnley
- *Skidamarink: A Silly Love Song to Sing Together*, by G. Brian Karas
- *Sam the Zamboni Man*, by James Stevenson, Harvey Stevenson
- *The Best Figure Skater in the Whole Wide World*, by Linda Bailey

Dramatic Creations: Winter Sports!

All children will participate in this guide drama. Children sit in a circle with plenty of room to move about. The teacher reads the actions and the children follow along.

Narrator: What a beautiful day for a toboggan ride! *(Children are seated in a circle facing clockwise. They place their hands on the shoulders of the person in front of them.)*

Narrator: Here we are at the top of the hill. Off we go! Everyone lean to the left. Everyone lean to the right. Duck your heads! Oh no! Here comes a snow bank! Everyone falls out of the toboggan! *(Children lay on the floor.)*

Narrator: What a beautiful day to go skiing! *(Children are standing in a circle facing clockwise.)* Move your arms back and forth as you ski along.

Narrator: We're at the top of the hill. Off we go! Everyone lean to the left. Everyone lean to the right. Duck your heads! Let's shush! *(Children crouch down low ready to fly down the hill).* Oh no! Here comes a huge pile of snow! Everyone jump!

Narrator: What a beautiful day to go ice fishing! *(Children are seated in a circle facing inward.)* Put your poles into the water. I think you've got a bite! Pull up to the left! Pull up to the right! Oh no! I think the fish got away. *(Children "fall" backwards.)*

Narrator: What a beautiful day to go skating! *(Children are standing in a circle facing clockwise.)* Put on your skates. Stand up tall. Let's skate around the rink. *(Children begin to skate in a circle.)* Now let's twirl to the left. Now let's twirl to the right. Do a jump! Take a bow. Let's skate back to where we started *(Children reverse their*

direction.) Oh no! Here comes a hole in the ice. Watch out! *(Children fall to the ground.)*

Narrator: What a beautiful day to go dog sledding! *(Children are seated in a circle facing clockwise.)* Hook up the dogs. Off we go! Lean to the left. Lean to the right. Duck your heads! Oh no! Here comes a snowy branch! Slow your dogs down. Stop them. Time to go back home!

Setting the Stage

Wintertime is more fun when children venture outside to make snow friends! Take the opportunity on a good snow-packing day to head to the playground to make new friends out of snow. Roll three balls of snow in three different sizes, add a hat and a scarf, and you've got a snow friend. Facial features can be hollowed out with fingers. Build an entire family out of snow! An alternative to the outdoor snow family is to build a model snow village in the classroom. Use a large table as the base for the model. Define the space by first using masking tape to identify the streets. Toy cars, busses, and fire engines will add to the realism of this miniature winter scene.

Have children use cartons of various sizes for houses, schools, a hospital, and office buildings. Use small boxes or cartons covered in differently colored construction paper for the buildings that you will need. Add doors and windows by using markers. Wooden craft sticks glued together make fences. Place the buildings along the streets. Have children create winter trees to line the avenues and dot the backyards of homes. Snip branches off from the dormant bushes and use play dough to anchor them on the table. Miniature, artificial evergreen trees will add some diversity to the landscape. Quilting batting cut in appropriate sizes will drape over the bases of the trees and on "lawns" to give the image of freshly fallen snow.

Create a sledding or ski hill by using boxes of various sizes. Arrange them in a pyramid, and then use heavy tagboard or cardboard to create the slopes. Cover with white felt or quilting batting. Miniature sledders will need sleds. Use wooden craft sticks and glue to create sleds to fly down the sledding hill. A blue piece of construction paper, cut in an oval, becomes a skating rink. Don't forget to build a warming shed near the rink! Build a snow fort using sugar cubes. Hold them together with white frosting. White packing peanuts and glue will serve the same purpose. Finally, add some snow friends. Build little snow people by using white play dough. Three balls of various sizes make the base, middle section, and the head. Strips of fabric scraps turn into scarves for our chilly friends. Milk jug caps can be used for their hats. Add facial features and buttons using small black beads. Place the snow friends in backyards, in the park near the sledding hill, or in the school playground. Anywhere you put these snow people will delight the young learners who created them.

Props and Supplies

large table, masking tape, boxes of varying sizes, construction paper, markers, small branches, play dough, wooden craft sticks, glue, quilting batting, toy vehicles, tagboard or cardboard pieces, white felt, toy people, sugar cubes, white frosting, packing peanuts, white play dough, fabric scraps, milk jug caps, and small black beads

Snow Friends (cont.)

Teacher Talk

- What kinds of buildings will you make for your snow scene?
- How will you divide the work to create the village?
- I wonder how you could make "snow angels" in this village.
- I wonder how your snow village will change as the weather warms up.

Literacy Connections

Songs and Fingerplays

Ten Little Snow Friends

(Sing to the tune "Twinkle, Twinkle, Little Star.")

Select ten children to dance in the center of the circle while the others are singing. One snow friend will be selected to "melt" with each verse. That child melts to the ground and then returns to their seat for the next verse. Make snowy headbands for the dancers by using light blue construction paper for the headband and the snowflake pattern on the **CD**.

Ten little snow friends,
Dancing all around,
Dancing all around,
Dancing all around.
Ten little snow friends
Dancing all around.
The sun came up
And one melts to the ground.

Nine little snow friends, and so on.

I Have a Little Snow Friend

(Sing this song using the eight notes in a scale: do, ray, me, fa, so, la, tee, do.)

Have children sing each line on one note of the scale, rising to the next note for the subsequent line. They begin on a low note and in a crouching position. As each line is sung, they move up the musical scale and also raise their body a bit, ending in an upright position. Sing the last line by reversing the scale and slowly returning from a standing position to the floor.

(do) I have a little snow friend.
(ray) He isn't very tall.
(me) He has a big fat middle.
(fa) His head is like a ball.
(so) He has a scarf to keep him warm.
(la) And a hat for fun.
(tee) But look the clouds are parting!
(do) Oh no! Here comes the sun!
Down, down, down, down, down, down, down, down!

The Snow Started Falling

The snow started falling,
One foot, two feet, three.
I put on my snow suit,
And I said with glee,
"It's time to build some snow friends!
See, the snow's just right!"
I built some little snow friends,
From morning until night.

Vocabulary Builders

New Words and Word Study: Playing in snow and making snow friends are fun ways to spend a day in the snow. Focus on words that my be unfamiliar like *slush, snowflakes, snow crystals, snowfall, blizzard, frost,* and *icicles.*

Onset/Rime: Words that have the same spelling pattern as the word *snow*.

/ow/ low, mow, row, blow, snow, throw, tow, sow, show, crow

Write All About It!

My Snow Friend Class Book

Have each child use white construction paper circles glued onto a blue construction paper background to create a snow friend. Use markers to create facial features and scraps of fabric for the scarf and hat. Once the snow friends are finished have children dictate or write the patterned text *(Child's name)'s snow friend is _____.* Children add descriptive words to complete the sentence such as funny, tall, skinny, friendly, and so on. Display art work on a bulletin board. When it's time to take them down, bind the pages together in a class book.

Book List

- *All You Need for a Snowman*, by Alice Schertle, Barbara Lavallee
- *Frosty the Snow Man*, Retold by Annie North Bedford
- *Snowballs*, by Lois Ehlert
- *The Jacket I Wear in the Snow*, by Shirley Neitzel
- *Katy and the Big Snow*, by Virginia Lee Burton
- *Snowy Day*, by Ezra Jack Keats
- *Elmer in the Snow*, by David McKee
- *Snow Joe*, by Carol Greene, Paul Sharp
- *Caps, Hats, Socks, and Mittens: A Book About the Four Seasons*, by Louise Borden, Lillian Hoban
- *Snowmen at Night*, by Caralyn Buehner, Mark Buehner
- *Stranger in the Woods: A Photographic Fantasy*, by Carl R. Sams
- *Flannel Kisses*, by Linda Crotta Brennan
- *Winter Friends*, by Carl R. Sams

Snow Friends (The End)

Dramatic Creations: Let's Build Snow Friends!

Two friends build snow friends and hurry to finish before the sun comes out and warms things up! Each snow person requires three children. Each of these three children enter the scene by doing summersaults into the center of the circle under the watchful eyes of the two builders.

The child who is the bottom part of the snow friend sits on the floor once he or she has rolled into the middle of the circle area. The child who is the middle part of the snow friend is on his or her knees just behind the "bottom" snow ball. The "head" will stand behind the other two.

The snow-friend builders supply the three-person snow-friend team with white poster board circles, which are decorated to resemble a snow friend. As each of the snow-friend actors is in position, they will be handed their white circle to hold.

All of the actors will follow the narrator's directions.

Narrator: One day two friends decided to go to the park and build a snow friend. They saw some snow that was just right for packing and rolling into big, big snowballs. They rolled the bottom snowball *(enter first child)*. Then they rolled a second, slightly smaller ball for the middle *(enter second child)*. Finally, they rolled the head, which was an even smaller snowball *(enter third child)*.

Two Builders: This is a perfect snow friend. Let's build another.

Narrator: So the two friends rolled another large snowball for the bottom. Then they rolled a middle sized snowball. And then they rolled the snowball for the head. *(Three children enter as directed above.)*

Two Builders: This is a perfect snow friend. Let's build another.

Narrator: So the two friends rolled another large snowball for the bottom. Then they rolled a middle sized snowball. And then they rolled the snowball for the head. *(Three children enter as directed.)*

Two Builders: This is a perfect snow friend. Let's build another.

Narrator: But before they could, the sun came out. *(A child enters holding a yellow "sun").*

Two Builders: Oh no!

Narrator: And right before their eyes, their three perfect snow friends began to melt, and melt, and melt. Soon they were just three puddles on the ground.

Props and Supplies

black adult-sized tee shirts, white fabric, white blankets, paper, paper clips, fishing line, scooter boards, blue tarp, small slide, paper fish, and white plastic eggs

Setting the Stage

Take a wintertime trip to the coldest continent on earth, Antarctica! That's where the Emperor Penguins play, the largest of the penguin species. Emperor Penguins are flightless and are great swimmers. Also, the father penguin cares for the egg while the mother penguin catches food. When the chick hatches, both the mother and father penguins take turns caring for the young. Many zoos have penguin exhibits excellent for field trips. Create a penguin colony in the classroom where children can be the penguins themselves!

Make Emperor Penguin costumes using black adult-sized tee shirts. Cut a large piece of white fabric or felt for the "bib," which covers most of the front of the penguin. Sew or use hot glue to attach the white fabric onto the front of the tee shirts. Once the children are suited up in their penguin costumes, let the play begin. Penguins enjoy the frosty land, where they make their home, as well as swimming in the arctic waters, where they find their food. Use white blankets for the snowy land. Lay them down on the floor in a corner of the room. Penguins find it difficult to travel quickly by walking. Their solution is to glide along on their bellies. Provide scooter boards so your penguins can glide along, too.

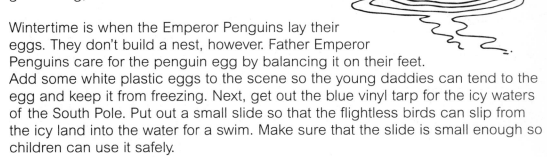

Wintertime is when the Emperor Penguins lay their eggs. They don't build a nest, however. Father Emperor Penguins care for the penguin egg by balancing it on their feet. Add some white plastic eggs to the scene so the young daddies can tend to the egg and keep it from freezing. Next, get out the blue vinyl tarp for the icy waters of the South Pole. Put out a small slide so that the flightless birds can slip from the icy land into the water for a swim. Make sure that the slide is small enough so children can use it safely.

Have children make fish for the ocean waters out of paper, decorating on both sides. Laminate for long-term use. Once in the water the penguins can swim on their bellies and gobble up fish for dinner. Make sure that the mama penguins bring some fish back to the daddies who are keeping the penguin eggs warm. Once the eggs hatch, both the mother and father penguins can go for swims to catch fish for their young and to catch dinner for themselves!

Decorate this corner of the room by hanging paper snowflakes from the ceiling. Young children can cut the snowflakes by folding the paper into quarters and then snipping along the folds. Use fishing line and paper clips to suspend the snowflakes in midair.

- I wonder how the penguins stay warm at the South Pole.
- How many fish do you think you will catch today?
- I wonder why the daddy penguin watches the egg instead of the mommy penguin.
- How far do you think penguins can swim?
- How long can they stay in the freezing water?

Literacy Connections

Songs and Fingerplays

Penguins, Penguins Fingerplay

Penguins, penguins slip and slide.
Penguins, penguins waddle by.
Penguins, penguins dressed so nice.
Penguins, penguins on the ice.
How many penguins take a dive?
One, two, three, four, five!

Have You Ever Seen a Penguin?
(Sing to the tune "Have You Ever Seen a Lassie?")

Have you ever seen a penguin, a penguin, a penguin,
Have you ever seen a penguin slide on the ice?

Slide this way and that way and this way and that way.
Have you ever seen a penguin slide on the ice?

Other verses:
Have you ever seen a penguin swim in the sea?
Have you ever seen a penguin catch a big fish?
Have you ever seen a penguin waddle around?

Where Are the Penguins?
(Sing to the tune "Where Is Thumbkin?")

Papa Penguin, Papa Penguin
Where are you? Where are you?
I am watching our chick.
Keeping warm on ice thick.
Warm him up! Warm him up!

Mama Penguin, Mama Penguin
Where are you? Where are you?
I am swimming in the sea,
Catching fish for you and me.
Now let's eat! Now let's eat!

Baby Penguin, Baby Penguin
Where are you? Where are you?
I am on the snowy land,
Holding onto daddy's hand.
Nice and safe! Nice and safe!

102   1-57029-533-6 *Year 'Round Dramatic Play*

Literacy Connections (cont.)

Vocabulary Builders

New Words and Word Study: The concept of the South Pole and Antarctica will go beyond most young children. However, their familiarity with penguins from the zoo and from books will create a framework for learning new vocabulary they will hear in this section. Focus on words like *arctic, frosty, icy, ocean, freezing, dive, waddle, chick, hatch,* and *colony.*

Onset/Rime: Words that have the same spelling pattern as the word *ice.*

/ice/ dice, mice, nice, rice, price, slice

Write All About It!

I Went Diving into the Sea Class Book

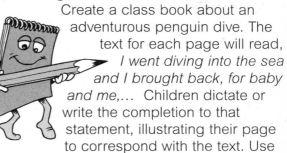

Create a class book about an adventurous penguin dive. The text for each page will read, *I went diving into the sea and I brought back, for baby and me,...* Children dictate or write the completion to that statement, illustrating their page to correspond with the text. Use dark blue construction paper for the background, and crayons or tempera paint for the illustrations.

Book List

- *Penguins!*, by Gail Gibbons
- *The Emperor's Egg*, by Martin Jenkins, Jane Chapman
- *Little Penguin's Tale*, by Audrey Wood
- *A Penguin Pup for Pinkerton*, by Steven Kellogg
- *Counting Penguins*, by Betsey Chessen, Pamela Chanko
- *The Little Penguin*, by A. J. Wood, Stephanie Boey
- *Puffins Climb, Penguins Rhyme*, by Bruce McMillan
- *Plenty of Penguins*, by Sonia W. Black
- *Penguin Dreams*, by J. Otto Seibold
- *Antarctic Antics: A Book of Penguin Poems*, by Judy Sierra
- *Penguins*, by Joy Labrack
- *Penguins 123*, by Kevin Schafer
- *Penguins ABC*, by Kevin Schafer

Dramatic Creations: A Penguin Colony

Guide children through this drama about life at the South Pole in an Emperor Penguin colony. All children stand in a circle as the drama begins. They act out the directions given to them by the narrator.

Penguins are very social animals. Thousands of penguins live together in a colony. Before you begin this drama, learn about penguins and how they behave. Examine their physical appearance and ask children: *How do penguins move about? If you were to walk like a penguin, what would that look like? How should you hold your arms to be more like a penguin?* Practice taking a few penguin walks!

Narrator: One cold and sunny winter's day, all of the penguins in the colony came together. They decided to go for a walk. First they walked to the right. *(Children penguin walk in a clockwise direction.)* Then they walked to the left. *(Children reverse direction.)*

But, walking was hard. They got down on their bellies and scooted across the icy ground. *(Children move on their bellies in a clockwise circle.)* That was more fun!

The all moved to the center of the ice and stood up again. It was time to take care of the eggs. The daddy penguins balanced the egg on their feet, *(Boys each have a plastic egg and balance it on their feet.)* while the mommy penguins went diving into the sea to find some fish. *(Girls go diving.)*

The daddy penguins stayed close together to keep warm. They stood very still so the eggs would not fall onto the ice. Soon, the mommy penguins came back with some fish. They waddled up to the daddies and gave them something to eat. *(The girls have brought back some paper fish.)*

Then, it was time for the daddy penguins to go for a swim. They will catch and eat more fish, and bring some back to the mommies.

The eggs are hatching. Now it is time for all of the penguins to go for a swim. They love the water.

(All penguins go swimming.) Oh no! I think I see a Leopard Seal. They love penguins! Especially for dinner! It's time for the penguins to get out of the water and go back to the land. *(All penguins go back to land.)*

The penguins stand close together so they can stay warm and safe from the Leopard Seals. *(Penguins all gather in a group.)* The penguins stand very still so the Leopard Seal won't see them. It worked! The Leopard Seals are moving away. All of the penguins are safe again. Now it is time for a nap. The penguins are tired. Close your eyes and go to sleep. Good night, penguins. Pleasant dreams! *(Penguins close their eyes and go to sleep.)*

It's in the Mail

Setting the Stage

We receive mail from the Postal Service almost everyday. Create a mail center in the classroom where children pretend to be mail carriers, where they write letters and postcards, and send packages to one another via their own classroom mail service. There are several holidays during the winter months when we send and receive cards and packages. Create the opportunity for children to do so as well at school.

Set up the class postal system by first constructing a free standing letter box using a large cardboard box. Cut a slit near the top of the box, and then have the children paint it red and blue. Paint the word *mail* on all sides. If the classroom is large enough, make and place several mailboxes in the classroom.

Create a post office for the young postal workers by using a free standing puppet theater as the counter. A multi-slotted cardboard shoe-storage unit will become the letter sorter. Assign each child in the classroom their own slot for the mail they receive. Take a photo of each child and place that photo, along with the children's written name, in their respective mail slots. The photo will help beginning readers make sure that the mail is going to the correct person. When the postal workers place the mail into the slots, they will match the name on the envelope to that of the name written on the mail slot.

Postal workers need some supplies. Provide them with a rubber stamp and washable ink stamp pad for canceling the postage stamps on the envelope. Mail carriers will need sacks for their mail as they go from mail box to mail box to collect the mail and bring it back to the post office.

Patrons will want to purchase stamps for their letters and packages. Have children create sheets of stamps for sale in the post office by running off the stamp template on the **CD** and having the children color them. Price them at one penny each and provide the children with pennies for the purchase of the stamps. Use a glue stick to hold the stamp in place on the envelope. Provide small cardboard packing boxes and some masking tape for the children to send packages through the mail as well.

Props and Supplies

large cardboard box, tempera paint (red, white, and blue), paint brushes, "junk" mail, free standing puppet theater, cardboard shoe-storage unit, rubber stamps, washable ink stamp pad, mail pouches, paper, envelopes, pattern for stamps on the **CD**, glue sticks, balance scale, small packaging boxes, tape, pennies, cash register

- What will you write in your letter?
- I wonder what happens to the letters once they go into the mailbox.
- Why do you think we need to put a stamp on letters?
- How do letters get to far away places?

Literacy Connections

Songs and Fingerplays

I Mailed a Letter Yesterday
(Sing to the tune "Pop Goes the Weasel.")

I mailed a letter yesterday.
I wrote it just for you.
I put it in the letter box,
On it's way to you.

(Repeat)

I mailed a letter yesterday.
I wrote it just for you.
Look inside your letter box,
It found its way to you.

First You Write a Letter
(Sing to the tune "Sing a Song of Sixpence.")

First you write a letter,
Sign it with your love.
Put it in an envelope,
A stamp goes up above.
Take it to the mailbox,
Be careful not to bend.
Off it goes with all the mail,
To your special friend.

Stamps
Use the postage stamp pattern on the **CD** to create the finger puppets for this fingerplay.

One stamp on the postcard,
Two stamps on the letter,
Three stamps on the package,
That contains a woolly sweater.

Four stamps on the small box,
Going far away.
Five stamps on the big box,
I'm sending off today.

Vocabulary Builders

New Words and Word Study: Children will be familiar with some aspects of the mail system. Stress non-gender specific titles when discussing these community helpers like *mail carrier*, *postal worker*, *letter carrier*. Other words and terms to use are *mailbox*, *mailbag*, *letter box*, *envelope*, *postage*, *stamps*, *packages*, *delivery*, and *route*.

Onset/Rime: Words that have the same spelling pattern as the word *send*.

/end/ bend, lend, mend, send, tend, spend

Write All About It!

Let's Write a Letter Class Book

To assemble this class book begin with a large sheet of construction paper for each child. Fold each paper on the short side, almost in half, leaving about 4 inches between each opposite end to create a pocket. Orient the folded paper so the 4-inch margin is on the left and the pocket opens to the top. Staple or glue two sides, leaving one side open to form the pocket.

On the pocket, have children write or dictate the following text: *(Child's name) drew a picture for _____.* On a separate sheet of paper, have the children draw a picture of their choosing. On the top of the picture, children write or dictate, *To _____* and *From (Child's name)*. Fold the picture and slip it into the pocket.

Bind the pages together to form a class book. Have children read the text on the pocket, remove the drawing, then return the drawing to the pocket, as in the story *The Jolly Postman*, by Allan Ahlberg.

Book List

- *The Post Office Book: Mail and How It Moves*, by Gail Gibbons
- *To the Post Office with Mama*, by Sue Farrell, Robin Baird Lewis
- *Day with a Mail Carrier*, by Jan Kottke
- *Mailing May*, by Michael O. Tunnell
- *Delivering Your Mail: A Book about Mail Carriers*, by Ann Owen, Eric Thomas
- *No Mail for Mitchell*, by Catherine Siracusa
- *Red-Letter Day: The Mail Carrier*, by Patricia Lakin, Doug Cushman
- *The Jolly Postman*, by Allan Ahlberg
- *Harvey Hare, Postman Extraordinaire*, by Bernadette Watts
- *Mail by the Pail*, by Colin Bergel, Mark Koeing
- *A Letter to Amy*, by Ezra Jack Keats
- *The Dove's Letter*, by Keith Baker
- *Corduroy Writes a Letter*, by Alison Inches, Allan Eitze

It's in the Mail (The End)

Dramatic Creations: The Mail Is Here!

It's time to say hello to the mail carrier and see what he or she has in the mailbag! One child plays the part of the mail carrier and delivers specific mail to six houses. The six houses are represented by six children, each holding a number from one to six on a piece of tag board. The mail carrier walks along and stops at each house. The narrator guides the action in this drama. The props needed are six house signs, each marked with a number 1–6, a mailbag, a letter labeled 1, a post card labeled 2, a large envelope labeled 3, a small package labeled 4, a magazine labeled 5, and a box labeled 6.

Narrator: The mail carrier was walking down the road. He/She came to house marked "Number 1." He/She had a letter to be delivered here.

Mail Carrier: I have a letter for you.

Child #1: This letter is from my mom. Thank you.

Narrator: The mail carrier walked down the street. He/She walked up to the house marked "Number 2." He/She had a postcard to be delivered there.

Mail Carrier: I have a post card for you.

Child #2: This letter is from my dad. Thank you.

Narrator: The mail carrier went to the house marked "Number 3." He/She had a large envelope to be delivered there.

Mail Carrier: I have a large envelope for you.

Child #3: This large envelope is from my grandma. Thank you.

Narrator: Then the mail carrier went to the house marked "Number 4." He/She had a small package to be delivered there.

Mail Carrier: I have a small package for you.

Child #4: This small package is from my grandpa. Thank you.

Narrator: The mail carrier walked down the street. He/She came to the house marked "Number 5." The mail carrier had a magazine to be delivered there.

Mail Carrier: I have a magazine for you.

Child #5: This magazine is from my friend. Thank you.

Narrator: The mail carrier was almost finished with his/her route. This was his/her last stop. He/She

had a box to be delivered there.

Mail Carrier: I have a box for you.

Child #6: This box is from my teacher. Thank you.

Narrator: The mail carrier had finished his/her route. He/She began to walk back to the post office. He/She passed house number six and waived.

Mail Carrier: See you tomorrow!

Child #6: See you tomorrow!

Narrator: He/She walked past house number five.

Mail Carrier: See you tomorrow!

Child #5: See you tomorrow!

Narrator: He/She walked past house number four.

Mail Carrier: See you tomorrow!

Child #4: See you tomorrow!

Narrator: He/She walked past house number three.

Mail Carrier: See you tomorrow!

Child #3: See you tomorrow!

Narrator: He/She walked past house number two.

Mail Carrier: See you tomorrow!

Child #2: See you tomorrow!

Narrator: He/She walked past house number one.

Mail Carrier: See you tomorrow!

Child #1: See you tomorrow!

Narrator: And with that, the mail carrier walked back to the post office, took off his/her mailbag, and went home.

Winter Art Activities

Winter Tree: Have children use crayons on light blue construction paper to draw the trunk and branches of a winter tree. Ask them to add snowflakes by using the end of an empty spool of thread. Peel back and clean off all of the paper on the end of a spool. Most spools have a six-sided design on the end, the same number of sides as a real snowflake! Use the cleaned end to print snowflakes onto the paper by dipping into paint. Children may also use small pieces of natural sponge for snowflake painting. Natural sponge has larger holes and will create an airier feeling to the painting.

Winter Class Tree: Use the sponge-painting technique on this large class tree as well. Provide the children with a 6' piece of butcher paper. Draw an outline of a trunk and branches. Have children use brown tempera paint to fill in the outline. Once dry, add the snowflakes by using the end of a spool of thread dipped in white tempera paint, or use natural sponges for stamping out the falling snowflakes. Snowflakes may also be added by tearing small pieces of white tissue paper and gluing them onto the butcher paper.

Soap Flake Snow Friends: Add water to laundry soap flakes. Mix to modeling consistency. Guide children in using the mixture to make three small snowballs in graduated sizes for their snow friend. Before the soap flake mixture hardens, children insert small craft beads, seeds, or buttons for facial features and buttons down the front. Tie a scrap of flannel for a scarf and use a milk jug cap for the hat. Add arms using twigs or short lengths of pipe cleaners. Turn a short piece of pipe cleaner into a broom with yarn "straw" twisted onto the end of the broom.

Snow Storm Paintings: Ask children to use crayons to draw a picture of a winter activity onto blue construction paper. Once the drawing is complete, have children create a snowstorm using a paintbrush and some water with Epson Salts. Dissolve about 1/4 cup of Epson Salts to 4 cups of water for the winter wash. Encourage children to brush this on in a swirling motion to resemble blowing snow. Let dry and see the swirling snowstorm! This mixture can also be used to paint onto glass. When it dries you will see lots of crystals.

Marvelous Mittens: Cut a piece of clear sticky paper into a 16" by 6" rectangle. Score it along the middle so it measures 8" by 8" when folded. Remove half of the paper backing to expose the sticky side. Have children place glitter, snips of yarn, small pieces tissue paper, colored cellophane, or sequins onto the sticky side. Once it has been decorated, remove the remaining paper backing and fold it over onto the decorated side. Next, cut a mitten shape no larger than 8" by 6" from the center of a piece of construction paper measuring 9" by 7", which will serve as a mitten "frame" for the decorated sticky paper. Place the glittery creation onto the frame and secure with tape. Hang in a window as a mitten sun catcher.

More Winter Fun
Book List for Winter

- *Animals in Winter*, by Henrietta Bancroft
- *Winter on the Farm*, by Laura Ingalls Wilder
- *Winter*, by Patricia Whitehouse
- *It's Winter*, by Jimmy Pickering
- *Winter Story*, by Jill Barklem
- *When Winter Comes: A Lullaby*, by Nancy Van Laan
- *White Snow, Bright Snow*, by Alvin R. Tresselt
- *Frog in Winter*, by Max Velthuijs
- *Big Snow*, by Berta Hader
- *Footprints in the Snow*, by Cynthia Benjamin, Jacqueline Rogers
- *Midnight in the Mountains*, by Julie Lawson, Sheena Lott
- *Winter, Awake*, by Linda Kroll, Ruth Lieberherr
- *White Wonderful Winter*, by Elaine W. Good, Shenk Susie Wenger

Flannel Board Props

Create felt pieces for children to use on a flannel board while exploring the following dramatic play themes.

The Toy Store: various toys such as tops, yo-yos, dolls, trains, building blocks, teddy bears, cars, and so on, and a toy box

Wrap It Up!: Laminate gift-wrapping paper which has been glued onto tagboard and then cut out into box shapes. Glue felt onto the backs of these squares so that the gift package can be applied to the felt board. Use sticky back bows in a similar manner. Make gifts to hide under the boxes and an evergreen tree.

Trim a Tree: large green evergreen tree, holiday decorations, star for the top of the tree, candles, birds, popcorn strings, bird feeders and snowflakes

Five candles are needed for the children in order to act out "Five Little Candles" fingerplay from the songs and fingerplay section.

Where Are the Bears?: bears in various sizes for the bear family in the "Are You Sleepy?" song, bear cave, winter trees with snow, snowflakes

The song "Ten Little Bears" requires just that, ten bears!

Winter Sports: ski and sledding hill, ice rink, people, winter clothing, ice skates, hockey sticks, skis, sleds, winter trees, snow, and snowflakes

Snow Friends: white circles in many sizes so that children can assemble their own snow friends, shapes for the eyes, nose, mouth, and buttons, fabric scraps for the scarf, several hats, arms, a broomstick, snow and snowflakes

Make ten assembled snow friends for the children to sing "Ten Little Snow Friends" at the flannel board.

South Pole Adventure: black penguin silhouettes, white "bibs," eyes, eggs, ice flows, blue ocean water, leopard seals, and fish

It's in the Mail: envelopes, postcards, packages, stamps, mailboxes, large postal mail box, letter carrier mailbag, mail truck, sidewalks, houses, and people

Props and Supplies

large cardboard appliance boxes, black crepe paper streamers, tape, clothesline, child-sized chairs, large rolls of butcher paper, tempera paint, brushes, tagboard, paper plates, crayons, plastic headbands, felt, hot glue, face paint, child-sized brooms, play money, cash register, small zipper baggies, and snacks such as small crackers or cereal

Setting the Stage

We're going to the zoo! It's time to visit all of the exotic animals there. The zoo is a special place for many young children. Transform a corner of the classroom into your own zoo where children can pretend to be animals and zoo visitors. And by all means, feel free to feed these animals!

Designate areas of the classroom for the animal displays. Using the perimeter of the room will allow the space needed and yet not take over the entire room. For the animal cages, you will need large cardboard appliance boxes. Cut off almost all of one of the longest sides. To give the allusion of bars on the cage, tape black streamers from the top to the bottom of the opening. Give the animals a separate entrance/exit by cutting a door in another side of the box. If large cardboard appliance boxes are not available, create an open-air zoo by using clothesline to rope off the cage area from the spectator area. Tape the clothesline onto the backs of children's chairs to make this barrier.

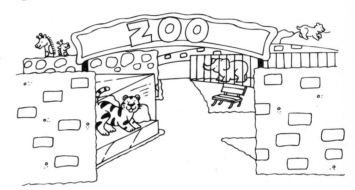

As a class, decide what kinds of animals there will be. Provide some comforts of "home" for the animals by doing research about their habitats, and then create painted backgrounds to correspond. For example, polar bears live in the arctic, so create a snowy scene. Monkeys will need trees to climb. Seals will want some water to swim in. Paint an ocean background and provide blue tarp for the "floor" of their exhibit.

Animal costumes can take different forms. Have children make masks using paper plates, which they have decorated accordingly. You can also reproduce masks on tagboard. Another option is to purchase headbands and glue felt ears onto them. Use little face paint for whiskers or other distinguishing facial features.

Once the costumes are made, it's time to put the animals in their cages and open the zoo for customers. Children take on the roles of zookeepers and visitors. The zookeepers need to feed the animals and clean their cages. Provide child-sized brooms for the cleaning. Patrons may also feed the animals. Set up a small stand where they may purchase little baggies of cereal or small crackers for the animals to nibble on.

We're Going to the Zoo (cont.)

- I wonder what kinds of food these animals eat.
- How do you think the animals feel about being in the zoo?
- I wonder what the animals are thinking when they see the people walk by.
- Do you think it would be fun to be a zoo keeper when you grow up?

Literacy Connections

Songs and Fingerplays

I'm Going to the Z-O-O
(Sing to the tune "La Cucaracha.")

I'm going to the Z-O-O.
I'm going with my mom.
And while we're there I want to share,
A peanut with an elephom. Elephom?

I'm going to the Z-O-O.
I'm going with my dad.
And while we're there I want to share,
A peanut with an elephad. Elephad?

I'm going to the Z-O-O.
I'm going with my sis.
And while we're there I want to share,
A peanut with an elephis. Elephis?

I'm going to the Z-O-O.
I'm going with my uncle.
And while we're there I want to share,
A peanut with an elephunkle. Elephunkle?

I'm going to the Z-O-O.
I'm going with my aunt.
And while we're there I want to share,
A peanut with an elephant! That's right!

Did You Ever See a Monkey?
(Sing to the tune "Have You Ever Seen a Lassie?")

Did you ever see a monkey, a monkey, a monkey?
Did you ever see a monkey,
Climb up a tree?

Climb this way and that way and this way and
that way,
Did you ever see a monkey climb up a tree?

Other verses:
Did you ever see an elephant
Spray with his trunk?

Did you ever see a buffalo
Stomp with his hoof?

Did you ever see a penguin
Waddle on the ice?

Did you ever see a lion
Roar big and loud?

Five Little Monkeys
Children will create monkey finger puppets for this fingerplay by using the pattern on the **CD**.

Five little monkeys swinging in the tree.
The first one said, "Hey, look at me!"
The second one said, "I'm going to get a treat."
The third one said, "Here's a banana you can eat."
The fourth one said, "Let's make some funny faces."
The fifth one said, "Come on my friends, I'll race ya."
So they all raced around the monkeys' pen,
They swung in the trees, then they raced around again.

Vocabulary Builders

New Words and Word Study: The zoo is a favorite place for many children to visit; however, don't assume that all children have visited one or are familiar with how zoos operate. Focus in on related words such as *zoo, zookeeper, cages, exhibits, displays, endangered animals, protect,* and *visitor.*

Onset/Rime: Words that have the same spelling pattern as the word *zoo.*

/oo/ boo, coo, goo, moo, zoo, shoo, too

Write All About It!

A Trip to the Zoo Class Book

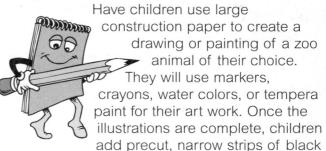

Have children use large construction paper to create a drawing or painting of a zoo animal of their choice. They will use markers, crayons, water colors, or tempera paint for their art work. Once the illustrations are complete, children add precut, narrow strips of black construction paper to resemble the bars of a cage. Finally, add the predictable text, *At the zoo, (child's name) saw a/an_____.* Once this work is finished, display the writing in the classroom, positioning them side by side. As the children view the animal artwork, they can pretend that they are taking a stroll through the zoo. Once the pictures are ready to come down, bind the pages together in a class book.

Book List

- *Curious George Visits the Zoo*, by Margret Rey, Alan J. Shalleck
- *If I Ran the Zoo*, by Dr Seuss
- *1, 2, 3 to the Zoo*, by Eric Carle
- *Zoo-Looking*, by Mem Fox, Candace Whitman
- *Zoo*, by Gail Gibbons
- *My Visit to the Zoo*, by Aliki
- *Polar Bear, Polar Bear, What Do You Hear?*, by Bill Martin Jr., Eric Carle
- *The Mixed-Up Chameleon*, by Eric Carle
- *Trip to the Zoo*, by Karen Wallace
- *Edward the Emu*, by Sheena Knowles
- *Patrick's Dinosaurs*, by Carol Carrick
- *Going to the Zoo*, by Tom Paxton
- *My Trip to the Zoo*, by Mercer Mayer
- *Be Nice to Spiders*, by Margaret Bloy Graham
- *Sam Who Never Forgets*, by Eve Rice
- *Color Zoo*, by Lois Ehlert

1-57029-533-6 *Year 'Round Dramatic Play*

We're Going to the Zoo (The End)

Dramatic Creations: Going to the Zoo

In this drama, three children take a trip to the zoo where they see several animal exhibits. You may choose to divide the remaining children into four groups and have each group act out the behaviors of a specific animal, or have all of the children participate in the animal actions each time. The "animals" will listen to the narrator's directions and act out the behaviors accordingly.

Child #1: Today is a good day to visit the zoo.

Child #2: Yes, let's go to the zoo.

Child #3: Me too!

Narrator: So the three friends got into the car and went to the zoo.

Child #1: I want to see the monkeys.

Child #2: Yes, let's see the monkeys.

Child #3: Me too!

Narrator: So they walked over to the monkey cage and watched the funny monkeys as they scratched themselves, as they ate bananas, and as they made funny faces.

Child #1: I want to see the tigers.

Child #2: Yes, let's see the tigers.

Child #3: Me too!

Narrator: The walked to the tiger cage. There they saw the sleeping tigers. They saw the stretching tigers waking up from their naps. They heard the roaring tigers! They watched as the tigers went back to sleep again.

Child #1: I want to see the snakes.

Child #2: Yes, let's see the snakes.

Child #3: Me too!

Narrator: They went to the snake exhibit next. They saw the snakes coiled up into a ball. They saw the snakes slither about. They saw the snakes stick out their tongues! They saw the snakes curl up and take a nap.

Child #1: I want to see the elephants.

Child #2: Yes, let's see the elephants.

Child #3: Me too!

Narrator: They hurried over to the elephant ring. They saw the elephants standing on their hind legs with their trunks high in the air. They saw the elephants eating peanuts with their trunks. They saw the elephants sucking up some water with their trunks. Oh no! They felt the cold wet spray from the elephants' trunks!

Child #1: I want to go home.

Child #2: Yes, let's go home.

Child #3: Me, too!

Narrator: So the three friends got back in the car and went home. They had a good day at the zoo!

The Pet Shop

Setting the Stage

Many families have pets. They are a part of the everyday life for many young children and a part of their families. Those children who do not have pets have probably thought that they would like one! Pets can be fun, but pets require lots of love and care. They are a big responsibility. Dramatic play centered on pets and the pet store will give child pet owners an opportunity to act out what they already know about pets. For those children who don't own a pet, the pet store will give them a chance to own the pet they've always wanted.

Provide children with a wide variety of stuffed animals for their pet shop. Children who bring their stuffed animals in from home will want to make sure that they are labeled! The animals will need cages to live in at the pet shop. Use real dog/cat kennels or make your own kennels using cardboard boxes. Birds will need cages as well, and so will the turtles, snakes, and hamsters. Each type of animal needs a cage specific to its needs. Try and find real cages for these animals as well. If none are available, use cardboard boxes. Have children add the necessary extras, such as bird swings out of short pieces of dowel and strings, hamster wheels out of a "slice" of a cylindrical oatmeal box, hamster tunnels out of cardboard paper tubes, and so on.

Each of the animals in the pet shop will need tender loving care, and that includes providing something to eat. Place plastic containers of various sizes in the cages for the animals to use as food and water dishes. Line the cages with newspapers like you might find in a real pet shop. The pets will want something to play with while they are at the pet store. Bring in clean plastic dog and cat toys for their amusement. Customers will want to purchase dog and cat toys as well. Set up a display for them to make their selections. Have children make pet supplies to sell.

The furry pets will need to be groomed, so they can look their best for the customers. Set up a grooming station using a table with a plastic tub, empty plastic shampoo bottles, an unplugged blow dryer, and brushes and combs for the finishing touches. Add some ribbons to make some pretty bows for the pets after their grooming is finished. Once the customers make their selection, have them use play money to pay for their purchase at the pet shop. The pet shop owner puts the money into the cash register.

Props and Supplies

stuffed animals, cages such as dog kennels, birdcages, acrylic fish tanks, plastic fish, plastic food dishes, carrying cases, plastic dog and cat toys, cardboard boxes, play money, a cash register, and grooming supplies such as brushes, tables, plastic tubs, empty bottles of shampoo, unplugged blow dryers, and ribbon

1-57029-533-6 *Year 'Round Dramatic Play*

- Do these animals have names?
- How will the new owners know how to take care of their new pets?
- How will the customers carry their new pets home with them?
- I wonder which pet most people would like best.

Literacy Connections

Songs and Fingerplays

Where Is Puppy?
(Sing to the tune "Where Is Thumbkin?")

Where is puppy? Where is puppy?
Here I am, here I am.
You have found a new home
Never more will you roam.
Here we go. Here we go.

Other verses:
Where is kitty?
Where is fishy?
Where is hamster?
Where is parakeet?
Where is slithery snake?

Take Me Down to the Pet Shop
(Sing to the tune "Take Me Out to the Ball Game.")

Take me down to the pet shop.
Let me look at the pups,
Kitties, and hamsters, and swimming fish.
I want a pet and I wish and I wish
That I had a pet that was my own.
One I could care for and love.
I want one, two, three little pets,
At the old, pet shop.

D-O-G-G-Y
(Sing to the tune "B-I-N-G-O.")

I went to the pet shop to buy a pet.
And I brought home a doggy
D-O-G-G-Y
D-O-G-G-Y
D-O-G-G-Y
And I brought home a doggy.

(Continue with additional verses until all letters in D-O-G-G-Y are clapped.)

Other verses:
And I brought home a kitty
And I brought home a snake
And I brought home a fishy

Vocabulary Builders

New Words and Word Study: Dogs, cats, and goldfish are common pets for many children. Some other animals might not be as familiar to them. Through conversation, learn what those might be and focus in on those animal names. Provide labeled pictures of those kinds of animals so that children can learn what they look like. Other words to use: *pet shop, groom, owner, purchase,* and *responsibility.*

Onset/Rime: Words that have the same spelling pattern as the word *dog.*

/og/ dog, fog, hog, jog, log, frog, bog

Write All About It!

The Best Pet Class Book

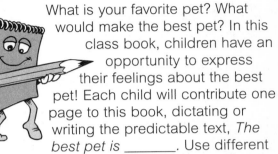

What is your favorite pet? What would make the best pet? In this class book, children have an opportunity to express their feelings about the best pet! Each child will contribute one page to this book, dictating or writing the predictable text, *The best pet is _____.* Use different mediums for the illustrations in the book such as crayon or marker drawings, colored pencils, tempera paints, or animal pictures cut from magazines.

Book List

- *Mrs. Katz and Tush*, by Patricia Polacco
- *The Best Pet of All*, by David LaRochelle, Hanako Wakiyama
- *Harry the Dirty Dog*, by Gene Zion
- *Good Dog, Carl*, by Alexandra Day
- *Slithery Jake*, by Rose-Marie Provencher
- *I Need a Snake*, by Lynne Jonell
- *Pick a Pet*, by Diane Namm, Maribel Suarez
- *Danny and the Dinosaur*, by Syd Hoff
- *Clifford's Kitten*, by Norman Bridwell
- *Kipper and Roly*, by Mick Inkpen
- *Bathtime for Biscuit*, by Alyssa Satin Capucilli
- *Mr. Putter & Tabby Walk the Dog*, by Cynthia Rylant
- *Frannie And Pickles: Frannie And Pickles*, by Preston McClear
- *Annie and the Wild Animals*, by Jan Brett
- *I Took My Frog to the Library*, by Eric A. Kimmel, Blanche Sims
- *Arthur's Pet Business: An Arthur Adventure*, by Marc Brown

Dramatic Creations: I Take Care of My Pet

Dogs are a typical pet in many homes. In this drama, children act out the necessary things to keep a dog happy and healthy. All children participate in this guided drama. Half of the children are the pet owners and the other half are the dogs. Pair children together: dog owner and pet. The narrator tells the story of how to take care of a dog. Both pet owner and pet respond to the narrator's directions by doing those things as told in the story.

Narrator: Having a dog is a big responsibility. Dogs must get a lot of exercise. They must be walked. *(Children walk in a circle, pet owners and dog partners walk side by side in a clockwise direction.)*

Dogs love to play fetch. *(Owners pretend to throw a ball to their pet. Dogs pretend to catch it.)*

Dogs love to roll in the grass. *(Dogs lie on their backs and roll around.)*

Sometimes when dogs roll in the grass they get dirty. It's time to go back home. *(Children walk in a counter clockwise direction and return "home.")*

The owner needs to give the dog a bath. *(Owners pretend to spray the dogs with a hose.)*

Sometimes dogs don't like that. They like to shake the water off! *(Dogs shake their fur dry.)*

Dogs like to bark. *(Dogs bark)* Sometimes their owners don't like that. They tell their pet "no." *(Owners say "no.")* The dogs love their owners so they listen and stop barking.

Dog owners need to feed their dogs. Put down a dish full of good food, just right for your pet. *(Owner pretends to put down a dish, dogs pretend to eat.)*

After dinner dogs need a good drink of water. *(Owners put down a pretend dish of water. Dogs pretend to lap up the water.)*

Now it's time for a nap. Everyone is tired from their walk and their bath. The owners find a comfortable place to lie down and they close their eyes. Their dogs need a nap, too. They find a comfortable place right next to their owners, and they lie down and close their eyes, too. Now everyone is sleeping.

Props and Supplies

stuffed animals, cages for them (such as small kennels or cardboard boxes), newspaper, towels, small plastic containers, hospital scrubs, white lab coats, toy doctor equipment (such as a stethoscope and thermometer), bandages, child-size chairs and a table, books, magazines, play money, cash register, big-wheel bike, tricycle, and wagon

Setting the Stage

Taking care of animals is a big responsibility. What do you do when your animal is sick? Call a veterinarian, of course! Give children the opportunity to take care of animals in need, either at the vet's office or out on the farm in this dramatic play section. Set up a veterinarian's office in a corner of the classroom. Bring in a variety of stuffed animals for the doctors to take care of. Each animal will need a cage in which to stay. Bring in small animal kennels or provide appropriately-sized cardboard boxes. Make the animals comfortable by lining each cage with newspaper or towels. Each animal will need food and water dishes as well. Small plastic containers work well.

A classroom table becomes an examining table for the veterinarians to use as they treat their patients. The doctors need to look the part as well. Provide scrubs or white lab coats for the vets to dress up in. Give the veterinarians the tools they need by providing toy doctor's equipment. A stethoscope and blood pressure cuff will help the vets to monitor their patients. Add a thermometer and a toy syringe to the vet's bag of tools. The veterinarians will see patients in their office. Set up children chairs for a waiting room. Provide books or magazines for the clients to read as they wait for their turn. The owners register with the receptionist, who will be seated at a child-sized table nearby. The receptionist escorts the pet owners into the examining room where they will see the veterinarian. When the office visit is over, the pet owner returns to the receptionist and pays for their visit. Provide play money and a cash register for the clients and the receptionist.

Veterinarians visit animals other places as well. Provide your vets with a classroom-appropriate vehicle so they can travel to see their patients. A big-wheel bike, tricycle, or wagon will work well. Vets travel to the farm to tend to horses, cows, pigs, and chickens. The veterinarians travel to the zoo to tend to the animals there. The young imaginations might have the veterinarians traveling to the jungle or the forest to look after the wild animals. Where they travel will depend on the types of stuffed animals that you provide.

Sort the animals into logical categories by asking children where they might find this particular type of animal. For example, "Where would we find a tiger?" Create the environments that the children suggest by their sorting criteria. Different corners of the classroom might become a farm, a jungle, a forest, or the zoo. Let their imaginations take them to these places!

The Veterinarian's Office (cont.)

- Do you think that pets like to go to the veterinarian's office?
- I wonder how the veterinarian and your doctor are alike.
- How does it make you feel to help animals?
- I wonder how you'll know what's wrong with the animals you treat.

Literacy Connections

Songs and Fingerplays

My Dog Had a Cough

(Sing to the tune "Hush Little Baby.")

My dog had a *(children "cough")* on a warm
   sunny day.
I went to the vet's office right away.
The vet said, "I'll help you."
He gave him a pill.
He fixed up my dog,
And he gave me the bill.

My cat had a *(children "sneeze")* on a warm
   sunny day.
I went to the vet's office right away.
The vet said, "I'll help you."
He gave him a pill.
He fixed up my cat,
And he gave me the bill.

My rabbit had the *(children "sniffle")* on a warm
   sunny day.
I went to the vet's office right away.
The vet said, "I'll help you."
He gave him a pill.
He fixed up my rabbit,
And he gave me the bill.

My bird had a *(children act out "chill")* on a warm
   sunny day.
I went to the vet's office right away.
The vet said, "I'll help you."
He gave him a pill.
He fixed up my bird,
And he gave me the bill.

I Went to the Farm

(Sing to the tune "Sing a Song of Sixpence.")

I went to the farm and what did I see?
A big brown cow that needed me.
She had a blade of grass stuck in her mouth.
I pulled it out, she gave a moo, and then she
   headed south.

I went to the zoo and what did I see?
A big grey elephant that needed me.
He had a bump upon his enormous trunk.
I fixed it up; he blew his trunk, and then went
   for a dunk.

I went into the jungle and what did I see?
A big bushy lion that needed me.
She had a sharp thorn stuck in her right claw.
I pulled it out, she gave a roar, and then she licked
   her paw.

I went into the forest and what did I see?
A big brown bear that needed me.
He had a stinger stuck in him, thanks to a bee.
I pulled it out, he gave a snort, and then climbed
   up a tree.

I went to my neighbor's and what did I see?
A big yellow dog that needed me.
She had her foot stuck in a little water pail.
I took it off, she gave a bark, and then she wagged
   her tail.

 1-57029-533-6 *Year 'Round Dramatic Play*

Literacy Connections (cont.)

Vocabulary Builders

New Words and Word Study: Young children love to try new words. The word *veterinarian* may be new to them. In addition, introduce familiar doctor words to them such as *patient, stethoscope, blood pressure cuff, thermometer, illness, cure, treated,* and *healed*.

Onset/Rime: Words that have the same spelling pattern as the word *cat*.

/at/ bat, cat, hat, mat, pat, flat, sat, fat, that, chat

Write All About It!

Going to the Vet's! Class Book

Have each child tell their own little story about taking a pet to the veterinarian's office in this class book. Illustrations should correspond with the predictable text. The text in this book will be, *(Child's name) took a/an _____ to the vet.* The children dictate or write the sentence filling in the blank by identifying a pet. Have children use crayons, markers, or tempera paint for their illustration.

Book List

- *Sally Goes to the Vet*, by Stephen Huneck
- *Hairy Maclary's Rumpus at the Vet*, by Lynley Dodd
- *I Want to Be a Vet* (I Want to Be (Firefly Paperback)), by Daniel Liebman, Dan Liebman
- *Caring for Your Pets: A Book About Veterinarians* (Community Workers), by Ann Owen, Eric Thomas
- *Animal Hospital*, by Judith Walker-Hodge
- *Good Dog, Paw!*, by Chinlun Lee
- *Milton Goes to the Vet*, by Hayde Ardalan
- *Mr. Betts and Mr. Potts*, by Rod Hull, Jo Davies
- *Pet Vet,* by Marcia Leonard, Dorothy Handelman
- *Help for Dear Dragon* (Modern Curriculum Press Beginning to Read Series), by Margaret Hillert
- *Barnyard Song*, by Rhonda Gowler Greene
- *Dr. Duck*, by H. M. Ehrlich
- *The Get Well Soon Book*, by Kes Gray, Mary McQuillan
- *Who's Sick Today?*, by Lynne Cherry

The Veterinarian's Office (The End)

Dramatic Creations: We're Going to the Veterinarian's Office

Guide children in assuming the roles of pet owners and pets. Have children play the pet owners, the pets named in this drama, and the vets. The pet should give the impression that he or she is ill. The pet goes with the owner to the vet's office, is treated there, and then leaves with a happy, spunky disposition. The narrator provides the direction for this visit to the vet's office.

Narrator: *(Child's name)* looked at her pet dog. Something was wrong.

Child #1: I think you are sick. Let's go to the vet.

Narrator: So *(child's name)* put her dog in the car and they drove to the veterinarian's office.

Vet: What's wrong?

Child #1: My dog is sick.

Vet: I can help. Here's some medicine.

Child #1: Thank you.

Narrator: So *(child's name)*) took her dog back home and everyone was happy.

Narrator: *(Child's name)* looked at her pet bird. Something was wrong.

Child #2: I think you are sick. Let's go to the vet.

Narrator: So *(child's name)* put her bird in the car and they drove to the veterinarian's office.

Vet: What's wrong?

Child #2: My bird is sick.

Vet: I can help. Here's some medicine.

Child #2: Thank you.

Narrator: So *(child's name)* took her bird back home and everyone was happy.

Narrator: *(Child's name)* looked at her pet snake. Something was wrong.

Child #3: I think you are sick. Let's go to the vet.

Narrator: So *(child's name)* put her snake in the car and they drove to the veterinarian's office.

Vet: What's wrong?

Child #3: My snake is sick.

Vet: I can help. Here's some medicine.

Child #3: Thank you.

Narrator: So *(child's name)* took her snake back home and everyone was happy.

Narrator: *(Child's name)* looked at her pet turtle. Something was wrong.

Child #4: I think you are sick. Let's go to the vet.

Narrator: So *(child's name)* put her turtle in the car and they drove to the veterinarian's office.

Vet: What's wrong?

Child #4: My turtle is sick.

Vet: I can help. Here's some medicine.

Child #4: Thank you.

Narrator: So *(child's name)* took her turtle back home and everyone was happy.

Narrator: The veterinarian had helped a dog, a bird, a snake, and a turtle. She was tired, so she went home. She was happy, too!

An additional song can be found on the CD.

1-57029-533-6 *Year 'Round Dramatic Play*

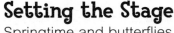

Props and Supplies

small fabric wings, fabric paint, strips of elastic, socks of various sizes, yarn, felt squares or similarly sized pieces of canvas, artificial greenery and flowers, tree branches, white plastic eggs, and ping-pong balls

Setting the Stage

Springtime and butterflies go hand in hand. In this season of new life, provide your children with the opportunity to act out this insect's life cycle beginning with the egg and moving through each of the unique phases of its life. Give children an understanding appropriate to their conceptual level of the life cycle of the butterfly.

Create a butterfly garden by providing artificial greenery and flowers. This is where butterflies will lay their eggs. Purchase small plastic eggs or use ping-pong balls to represent the butterfly eggs. The eggs will hatch and out emerges the larva, or caterpillar. Have children use child-sized socks on their hands to simulate the larva. Look at pictures of different kinds of butterfly larva. Many are colorful and striped, or have interesting looking "hairs" sticking out. Have the children use fabric paint and yarn to decorate their sock to resemble their favorite caterpillars. Once hatched the larva creeps and crawls along looking for food to eat. After the larva has eaten their fill, it's time to make the pupa, or chrysalis. The sock larva crawls into a larger sock suspended from a sturdy tree branch. It won't take long before the larva will turn into a beautiful butterfly.

Hand puppet butterflies are easy to make. Provide another sock for children to wear on their hand. Have them create felt wings, painting them to resemble their butterfly. Supply precut wings to the children. Use one felt square for each pair of wings. Guide children in squirting paint on one side of the wing, and then fold the wing over onto the other one creating a mirror image. At the center of the wings, cut small several slits in the felt. Make each slit parallel to the "body" of the butterfly. Cut two slits near the top of the butterfly's body and two cuts near its tail. Thread a strip of elastic through each slit and fasten the ends of each piece of elastic to make wristbands. Have children wear the butterfly wings on their wrist over the sock hand puppet. As children fly their butterflies, encourage them to move their arms up and down to allow for some lift on the felt wings. The butterflies will be landing on flowers and leaves along the way, but they don't eat them! They only drink water now. In time the cycle begins again. Little butterflies will be laying little white eggs in the greenery.

Of course, putting on wings and fluttering around the room will be fun, too. Supply the prop box with child-sized wings for them to use as well.

- I wonder how the little larva will know what to do once they've hatched.
- Do you think that larva has any predators?
- What happens to the butterflies in the winter?
- I wonder if there are certain flowers that butterflies prefer.

Literacy Connections

Songs and Fingerplays

The Larva's Lunch
(Sing to the tune "The Twelve Days of Christmas.")

On the first day the larva ate one big green leaf,
And then he took a nice long nap.

On the second day the larva ate two flower petals,
One big green leaf,
And then he took a nice long nap.

On the third day the larva ate three watermelons,
Two flower petals,
One big green leaf,
And then he took a nice long nap.

On the fourth day the larva ate four string beans,
Three watermelons,
Two flower petals,
One big green leaf,
And then he took a nice long nap.

On the fifth day the larva ate five ripe strawberries,
Four string beans,
Three watermelons,
Two flower petals,
One big green leaf,
And then he took a nice long nap.

(Add additional verses as desired.)

An additional song can be found on the CD.

One Butterfly
(Sing to the tune "Five Little Ducks.")

Guide children to create butterfly finger puppets to wear in this song. The patterns are on the CD.

One butterfly flew out one day,
In the merry month of May.
She flew over to the zoo,
Met a friend, and then there were two.

Two butterflies flew out one day,
In the merry month of May.
They darted past a flowery tree,
Met a friend, and then there were three.

Three butterflies flew out one day,
In the merry month of May.
They fluttered on over to the store,
Met a friend, and then there were four.

Four butterflies flew out one day,
In the merry month of May.
They floated over to a hive,
Met a friend and then there were five.

Five butterflies flew out one day
In the merry month of May.
They were having so much fun,
They didn't notice that day was done.

Five butterflies flew out one day,
In the merry month of May.
The were sleepy, it was dark,
They slept in a tree in the middle of the park.

Vocabulary Builders

New Words and Word Study: Butterflies are so beautiful to watch, and parts of their life cycle are evident as children find caterpillars and observe brightly colored butterflies. Focus on the scientific terms in this section, such as *egg, larva/caterpillar, pupa/chrysalis, butterfly, life cycle,* and *predators.* Other words to use are *flutter, emerge, change, land, antennae,* and *insect.*

Onset/Rime: Words that have the same spelling pattern as the words *spring* and *wing.*
/ing/ *king, ring, sing, wing, spring, swing, sting, bring*

Write All About It!

The Hungry Caterpillar Class Book

Create your own munching caterpillar book, similar to Eric Carle's *The Very Hungry Caterpillar*, and focus on numbers and the days of the week. Each of these small books will have seven pages. The text will read, *On Monday, the little caterpillar ate one (name one food item). On Tuesday, the litter caterpillar ate two (name two food items)* and so on.

Illustrations need to correspond to the number on each page. For example, *On Wednesday, the little caterpillar ate three bananas*, the illustration should show one caterpillar and three bananas. To make the caterpillars, use a washable green ink pad and the children own fingerprints lined up in a row! Washable black, fine-tipped markers will supply the legs, antennae, and facial features for their wiggly caterpillars. Bind the pages together in a sequential order, beginning with Monday and the number one.

Book List

- *From Caterpillar to Butterfly* (Let's-Read-and-Find-Out Science 1), by Deborah Heiligman
- *Good Night, Sweet Butterflies: A Color Dreamland*, by Dawn Bentley
- *Waiting for Wings*, by Lois Ehlert
- *Angelina and the Butterfly*, by Katharine Holabird
- *The Butterfly House*, by Eve Bunting, Greg Shed
- *Monarch Butterfly*, by Gail Gibbons
- *Where Butterflies Grow*, by Joanne Ryder, Lynne Cherry
- *The Butterfly Alphabet*, by Kjell B. Sandved
- *Born to Be a Butterfly*, by Karen Wallace
- *The Butterfly Alphabet Book*, by Brian Cassie
- *Memories of a Monarch*, by J. Elaine Senack
- *The Very Hungry Caterpillar*, by Eric Carle
- *Inch by Inch*, by Leo Lionni
- *Miss Hallberg's Butterfly Garden*, by Gay Bishop Brorstrom

Butterflies (The End)

Dramatic Creations: Life Cycle of the Butterfly

In this guided drama, each child needs a large towel or other piece of fabric in a similar size. Have them use this fabric as their prop in acting out the life cycle of the butterfly. The narrator directs the children's actions. The children begin by sitting in a circle. They are positioned in a tight ball with the towel wrapped around them.

Narrator: Sitting on the underside of a big leaf was a little insect egg. The egg was laid there by a butterfly. The egg was under the big leaf to give it some protection. The day came for the egg to hatch. It wiggled just a little, and then out from under the big leaf crawled a little larva. *(Children emerge from under the towel and wrap the towel snuggly around their shoulders and crawl about in a circle.)*

The larva was hungry. He ate and ate and ate and ate until his little belly was full and he had grown into a much larger larva. *(Children use their mouths to munch on pretend leaves.)*

The time came for the larva to begin the next part of his life. He began to make a pupa where he would quietly stay and wait for some changes. *(Children stand and wrap the towel around their upper body covering themselves.)*

Inside the pupa, things did begin to change. The larva wasn't feeling like a larva anymore. His body was growing. He looked less like a worm and more like a butterfly. *(Children are still standing and give a little wiggle.)*

Finally, it was time for the butterfly to emerge from its little home. First the butterfly stretched out his right wing, *(Children clasp one end of the towel in their right hand and extend their right arms.)* and

then it was time to stretch its left wing. *(Children clasp the other end of the towel in their left hand and extend their left arms.)*

The new butterfly looked at his wings in amazement! How could such a wonderful thing have happened to him? He gently flapped his right wing. He gently flapped his left wing. Then he flapped them both together. He was flying! The little butterfly took off and was flying in the air! *(Children flap their towel wings and gracefully move in a clockwise direction in the circle.)*

The butterfly moved so gracefully. He flew up and he flew down. He twirled around and around. He was getting tired. He flew to the nearest branch and rested. *(Children follow the narrator's directions.)*

A Bouquet of Flowers

Setting the Stage

Spring is a time of blossoms and gardens of planting and growing things. Bring a garden indoors for young horticulturists to practice their gardening skills. Ask children to pretend to plant seeds and care for their little plants, which grow into flowering plants. They will "pick" the flowers for delivery to a florist shop where beautiful bouquets are arranged for their customers.

To begin, set up a gardening table in a corner of the classroom. Provide plastic pots of various sizes for the gardeners to "plant" their seeds. Insert florist foam into the bottom of each container and secure it in place with hot glue. A little artificial moss on top of the foam will make the pots more attractive. Large "seeds," such as pinto beans, will be easy for little fingers to plant into the mossy pots. Cover the seeds with circles of brown felt for soil.

Have gardeners "water" their seedlings using small watering cans. In time the little seeds will give way to sprouting greenery. Provide some artificial greens for the children to insert into the florist foam. Have children add artificial flowers to their potted greenery. Make sure the plants are in a sunny space!

When the flowers are in full bloom, the gardeners can "pick" them and sell them in a florist's shop. Provide a table for the floral displays. Guide children in arranging and rearranging the flowers into pleasing bouquets for their customers. Add bows and other trimmings to make the flower arrangements even more attractive. Some of the customers in the florist's shop will want their bouquet wrapped. Show children how to place the flowers on tissue paper, wrap them, and then tie them with a ribbon. Provide a cash register for the florist shop and play money for the customers. Add a telephone so the florist can take phone orders. Guide children in writing the orders down on notepaper. Flowers for bouquets and plants will be delivered to the customer's home once the order is placed. For that, have children use a wagon to make their deliveries. Don't forget to make a sign for the side of the wagon!

Although bringing soil, seeds, and water into the classroom can be a bit messy, think about doing that alongside of the artificial greenery play. Children will soon see little blades of grass, or carrot tops poking out from planting soil nearby. Their play will mirror the real growing plants in the classroom.

Props and Supplies

artificial plants and flowers on individual stems and/or vines, plastic flowerpots, florist foam, artificial moss, brown felt circles, small watering cans, bows, ribbons, tissue paper, phone, note pad, pencil, cash register, play money, and a wagon

1-57029-533-6 *Year 'Round Dramatic Play*

- What kinds of plants do you think will grow from those seeds?
- I wonder how you'll arrange the flowers for your customers.
- Do you think that your customers will want delivery?
- What other things do you think you could sell in the florist shop?

Literacy Connections

Songs and Fingerplays

The Gardener Plants the Seeds

(Sing to the tune "The Farmer in the Dell.")

The gardener plants the seeds.
The gardener plants the seeds.
It's time to garden, it is spring.
The gardener plants the seeds.

The rain waters the seeds.
The rain waters the seeds.
It's time to garden, it is spring.
The rain waters the seeds.

The sun warms the soil.
The sun warms the soil.
It's time to garden, it is spring.
The sun warms the soil.

The sprouts begin to grow.
The sprouts begin to grow.
It's time to garden, it is spring.
The sprouts begin to grow.

The plants grow so big.
The plants grow so big.
It's time to garden, it is spring.
The plants grow so big.

It's time to pick the beans.
It's time to pick the beans.
It's time to garden, it is spring.
It's time to pick the beans.

Five Pretty Flowers

Have children make flower finger puppets using the pattern on the accompanying CD.

Five pretty flowers growing by the door.
One was picked and then there were four.
Four pretty flowers swaying in the breeze.
One was picked and then there were three.
Three pretty flowers in the morning dew.
One was picked and then there were two.
Two pretty flowers basking in the sun.
One was picked and then there was one.
One pretty flower was picked along the way.
He joined the others to make a nice bouquet!
(Show all five flowers again.)

An additional song can be found on the CD.

Literacy Connections (cont.)

Vocabulary Builders

New Words and Word Study: Plants and greenery in their many forms are abundant, but children might not be acquainted with the process of growing flowers for sale at a florist shop. Words to focus on are *florist, bouquet, flowers, blooms, blossoms, buds, stems, soil, seeds, arrangement, delivery, watering can,* and *sprouts.*

Onset/Rime: Words that have the same spelling pattern as the word *bud.*

/ud/ bud, cud, dud, mud, stud, thud

Write All About It!

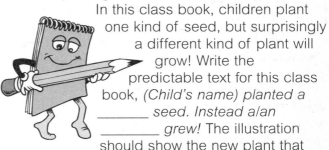

The Surprising Garden Class Book

In this class book, children plant one kind of seed, but surprisingly a different kind of plant will grow! Write the predictable text for this class book, *(Child's name) planted a _____ seed. Instead a/an _____ grew!* The illustration should show the new plant that grew in the garden. Use scraps of different colored construction paper, glued onto a pastel colored background. Have children use markers or crayons to add details to the construction paper foliage.

Book List

- *Whose Garden Is It?*, by Mary Ann Hoberman
- *This Year's Garden*, by Cynthia Rylant
- *A Gardener's Alphabet*, by Mary Azarian
- *My Day in the Garden*, by Miela Ford, Anita Lobel
- *The Garden Is Open*, by Pamela Pease
- *In My Garden: A Counting Book*, by Ward Schumaker
- *The Wind's Garden*, by Bethany Roberts
- *Tops & Bottoms*, by Janet Stevens
- *Flower Garden*, by Eve Bunting
- *Planting a Rainbow*, by Lois Ehlert
- *Muncha! Muncha! Muncha!*, by Candace Fleming, G. Brian Karas
- *The Carrot Seed*, by Ruth Krauss, Crockett Johnson
- *Growing Vegetable Soup*, by Lois Ehlert
- *Over in the Garden*, by Jennifer Ward, Kenneth J. Spengler
- *City Green*, by Dyanne DiSalvo-Ryan

Dramatic Creations: Spring Garden

Have children be flowers growing in a spring garden in this guided drama. The narrator gives the children direction as the script is read. All children participate as either flowers or gardener. Select one child to tend to the garden. The flowers will be identified by the color of their shirts, or have children wear a flower headband by using the flower pattern on the **CD**. The drama begins with the children seated in a circle and the gardener at the ready to tend the garden.

Narrator: Spring has just arrived. The snow is gone and the sun is shining bright. It is warming the earth. Gardener *(child's name)* goes out into his/her garden to check the soil.

Gardener: The soil is just right. It's not too wet, and it's not too dry.

Narrator: It's time to plant the seeds. First the gardener plants some white daisies.

(The gardener taps the shoulder of children wearing the white flower headbands, or white shirts. When tapped, those children bundle up into a tight ball on their knees ready to grow in the garden. With each color called, the gardener repeats his/her actions until all children are little seeds waiting to grow in the garden.)

The gardener plants some black and brown cosmos seeds. Then the gardener plants some yellow marigold seeds. Next, he/she plants some blue morning glory seeds. Then he/she plants some purple aster seeds. The gardener plants some orange poppy seeds. Then he/she plants some red and pink geranium seeds. Finally, gardener *(child's name)* plants some green eucalyptus seeds.

All of the seeds are planted in the soil. They need some things to grow! They need rain, *(Children make a "shhh" sound to represent rain.)* Sometimes when it rains there is lightening and thunder. *(Children make "boom" noises for thunder.)* When the rain shower has ended the birds

come out to splash in the puddles. *(Children make "tweet" noises for the birds.)* The sun is shining brightly again and the earth warms up. The seeds begin to grow.

(As each flower color is named, the gardener taps those children on the shoulder and those children stand.)

First the white daisies begin to grow. Then the black and brown cosmos grow. The yellow marigolds begin to grow. The blue morning glories begin to grow. Then the purple asters begin to grow. The orange poppies begin to grow. Then the red and pink geraniums begin to grow. Finally, the green eucalyptus begins to grow. The gardener looks around at his/her garden.

Gardener: What beautiful flowers.

Narrator: The gardener has an idea. He/She will gather a bouquet to bring home.

(As each color flower is named, the gardener brings those children into the center of the circle.)

First he/she gathers together the white daisies. Then the black and brown cosmos. The yellow marigolds are next. Then the gardener gathers the blue morning glories. Purple asters join the bouquet. The orange poppies are gathered together. The red and pink geraniums join the other flowers. Finally, the green eucalyptus finishes the bouquet.

Gardener: What a beautiful bouquet!

If You Build It...

Setting the Stage

Put on your hard hat and get out the tools; spring is a time for building things! Give children the opportunity to be builders as the dramatic play area is transformed into a workshop for busy little hands.

Begin by collecting small wood scraps, which are sanded smooth to avoid slivers. Use a plastic bin for storage. In a separate storage bin provide pieces of PVC pipe and fittings. Short pieces of pipe with 90-degree "elbows" will be fun for children to assemble into a variety of shapes. Make sure that the edges of these pieces are smooth as well. Also collect packing tape and sheets of cardboard cut into manageable sizes. Hard hats, safety goggles, and a carpenter's apron will give children the protection they need in this construction zone. Make sure that children understand the importance of this safety equipment and wear goggles and hard hats every time they are in the workshop.

Before carpenters or construction workers ever begin to build, they have a plan. Brainstorm what kinds of things they might build in the workshop, and then provide children with paper and pencils write ideas down. Encourage children to think about the materials they have and how they might be used. Children then write or draw a list of the materials they will use in the construction phase.

Have children use wood glue to assemble their creations. To keep the area clean, provide lots of plastic drop cloth and/or newspapers. Using many toy plastic tools, allows young carpenters to visit various job sites in the classroom. Have children pretend to repair and construct items of their interest. Give them the chance to practice their hammering skills by adding a log, large-headed nails, and lightweight hammers to the workshop. Set a two-foot-long log on end and children may begin to pound nails into it. Find soft wood if available, so the nails are easier to pound into the wood. As an alternative, provide sheets of thick Styrofoam and golf tees to pound. Remember to set the ground rules using tools, especially when children are using real hammers and nails. Limit the number of children who are using the pounding log. Carpenters need to clean up after a day in the workshop. Use brooms and dust pans to keep the floor clean. Provide sponges and mild sudsy water in small buckets to give the dusty surfaces a clean shine.

Props and Supplies

hard hats, safety glasses, tool belts, plastic toy tools, tape measures, sanded wood scraps, sandpaper, craft sticks, short pieces of PVC pipe and fittings, wood glue, paper, pencils or markers, Styrofoam sheets, golf tees, pieces of sturdy cardboard, packing tape, log slice, large head nails, lightweight hammers, caution tape, tempera paint, brushes, brooms, dust pans, sponges, water buckets, newspapers, and plastic drop cloths

Teacher Talk

- I wonder what you will build in the workshop today.
- Do you think you will have enough materials?
- How will you put the materials together?
- Are you going to work as a team with another carpenter to build something?
- Is there anything here that needs fixing?

Literacy Connections

Songs and Fingerplays

I'm Building a Wall
(Sing to the tune "The Farmer in the Dell.")

The tape measures the wood.
The tape measures the wood.
I'm building a wall, straight and tall.
The tape measures the wood.

The saw cuts the wood.
The saw cuts the wood.
I'm building a wall, straight and tall.
The saw cuts the wood.

The hammer pounds the nail.
The hammer pounds the nail.
I'm building a wall, straight and tall.
The hammer pounds the nail.

The screwdriver turns the screw.
The screwdriver turns the screw.
I'm building a wall, straight and tall.
The screwdriver turns the screw.

The broom sweeps the dust.
The broom sweeps the dust.
I'm building a wall, straight and tall.
The broom sweeps the dust.

The Three Little Houses

A house of straw was built for me,
A house outside of town.
A great big wind blew down on it,
And my house came tumbling down.

A house of sticks was built for me,
A house outside of town.
A great big wind blew down on it,
And my house came tumbling down.

A house of bricks was built for me,
A house outside of town.
A great big wind blew down on it,
And my house came tumbling down.

The three little pigs lived in that house,
The house made out of bricks.
They learned that when you build a house,
Bricks are stronger than straw or sticks.

I Have a Hammer and a Nail
(Sing to the tune "B-I-N-G-O.")

I have a hammer and a nail and with them I will pound,
P-O-U-N-D
P-O-U-N-D
P-O-U-N-D
And with them I will pound.

I have a hammer and a nail and with them I will pound,
Clap-O-U-N-D
Clap-O-U-N-D
Clap-O-U-N-D
And with them I will pound.

(Continue with additional verses until each letter has been eliminated.)

Vocabulary Builders

New Words and Word Study: Focus on words specific to the process of building. Words to use are *carpenters*, *construction workers*, *construction*, *building*, *workshop*, *materials*, *supplies*, *hammer*, *sandpaper*, *nails*, *protection equipment*, *safety*, *goggles*, and *hard hat*.

Onset/Rime: Words that have the same spelling pattern as the word *saw*.

/aw/ jaw, paw, saw, claw, draw, straw

Write All About It!

The House That I Built Class Book

Each child will become a carpenter with markers, tempera paint, crayons, scraps of construction paper, and glue in this class book. Encourage children to think about the different kinds of houses that they each live in. What color are they? How many stories tall? Do you live in an apartment house or a trailer? Look at pictures of different kinds of housing around the world. Perhaps children would like to "build" a house based on that information. Have children create a house and then add this predictable text, *This is the house that (child's name)* built. Bind the pages together for a class book.

Book List

- *Jobs People Do: A Day in a Life of a Builder*, by Linda Hayward
- *Katy No-Pocket*, by Emmy Payne, H. A. Rey
- *How a House Is Built*, by Gail Gibbons
- *Building a House*, by Byron Barton
- *Henry Builds a Cabin*, by D. B. Johnson
- *Lot at the End of My Block: Picture Book*, by Kevin Lewis
- *Building*, by Elisha Cooper
- *Albert's Alphabet*, by Leslie Tryon
- *The House That Jack Built*, by Diana Mayo
- *When I Was Built*, by Jennifer Thermes
- *Little House*, by Virginia Lee Burton
- *Construction Zone*, by Tana Hoban
- *Tool Book*, by Gail Gibbons
- *Three Little Pigs*, retold by James Marshall
- *The Three Little Pigs*, by Steven Kellogg

Dramatic Creations: The Three Little Kids

This drama will sound familiar to children as it is an adaptation of *The Three Little Pigs*. In this version, however, the Three Little Kids are up against the spring weather of wind and rain. Will their houses stand? Provide a large area for the children to act out this drama in which all children are involved.

Narrator: Once upon a time, there were three little kids. They each wanted to build their own house.

Child #1: I want a house of straw.

Child #2: I want a house of sticks.

Child #3: I want a house of bricks.

Narrator: So each of the kids set out to build their own house. The first little kid found some straw to build his/her house. *(Child #1 selects four other children to stand in a square with their hands held high and all joining together to form a roof.)* The second little kid found some sticks to build his/her house. *(Child #2 selects four other children to stand in a square with their hands held high and all joining together to form a roof.)* The third little kid found some bricks to build his/her house. *(Child #3 selects four other children to stand in a square with their hands held high and all joining together to form a roof.)*

Narrator: Once their houses were built, each little kid moved into their house. *(Children #1, #2, and #3 move into their new houses by sitting on the floor in the middle of their children house.)*

Child #1: I love my new house made of straw.

Child #2: I love my new house made of sticks.

Child #3: I love my new house made of bricks.

Narrator: Things were just fine until one day the clouds began to gather. The sky grew dark and there was a cool breeze in the air. *(Children in the audience begin to gently blow.)* The straw house shook. *(The straw house children wiggle, but still stand.)* The stick house shook. *(The stick house children wiggle, but still stand.)*

The brick house stood firm. Then the rain began to come. *(Children in the audience softly say "pitter patter.")* The straw house began to sag a bit. *(The straw house children begin to drop their arms.)* The stick house began to lean. *(The stick house children lean to one side, but still stand.)* The brick house stood firm.

Then the wind began to blow hard. *(Children in the audience blow forcefully.)*

The straw house began to topple. *(The straw house children sit on the floor.)* The first little kid was getting all wet. He/She went to the second little kid's house made of sticks.

Children #1: May I come in?

Children #2: Yes, you may.

Narrator: Now both of the little kids were safe and dry in the house made of sticks. But, the rain came harder and faster. *(Children in the audience say "pitter patter" a little louder and faster.)* The house made of sticks began to lean even further. Soon that house was on the ground. *(The stick house children sit on the floor.)* The two little kids went to the brick house.

Children #1 and #2: May we come in?

Child #3: There is no room here!

Narrator: The two little kids were clever. They had an idea. They went and got some more bricks *(Child #1 and #2 each select four children to make new houses.)* and they decided to build their own brick houses. They worked quickly and were soon inside their new homes safe and dry. Each little kid had a very sturdy house made of bricks.

Nests, Eggs, and Feathers

Props and Supplies

strips of fabric for making child-sized nests and for making bird wings, plastic headbands, craft feathers, hot glue, bathroom and/or paper toweling tubes, markers, crayons, elastic, adult-sized tube socks, plastic eggs, small beanbag-type stuffed birds, small craft pompons, pipe cleaners, Velcro™, binoculars, bird identification books, notepads, paper, plaster of paris, and generous fabric strips

Setting the Stage

Chirp, chirp! Spring is here, and so are the warm weather birds. Celebrate this sign of spring by providing opportunities for children to be a part this special time of spring.

Have children dress like birds by transforming empty cardboard bathroom tissue rolls into beaks. Keep one end of the tissue roll circular. That side will be worn against the child's face. Cut the other end of the tissue roll into a pointed beak, a round beak, or a short or long beak. Look at bird books to decide how to cut the beaks. Ask children to color the beaks with markers or crayons. Some birds have very long beaks. Use empty paper towel rolls for those beaks. Punch a hole on either side of the uncut end of each beak. Provide a length of elastic, thread both ends through the holes, and tie them securely in place. The elastic should be just a bit smaller than the circumference of your child's heads. Feathered headbands will be fun to wear to compliment the outfit. Purchase plastic headbands and hot glue craft feathers onto them. Wings are easy to make by taking adult-size tube socks and cutting off the toe. Sew or hot glue strips of fabric onto the socks. Have children pull their sock wings up onto their arms.

Our little feather friends are now ready to make nests. Provide generous strips of fabric for them to arrange their own personal, child-sized nests. Polar fleece, corduroy, lacy knits, or flannel are interesting and varied textures for the children to use. "Do not disturb" signs remind us to be quiet as the birds sit on their plastic eggs of varying colors and sizes. Once the eggs hatch, small beanbag-stuffed birds will reside in the nests while the mommy and daddy birds are busy finding food for their young. Babies will eat caterpillars made from small craft pompons glued together in a row, and garden worms made from pipe cleaners. Guide children in placing these around the room. When it's time to feed the babies, have birds fly off to find worms and caterpillars for their babies. A little piece of hook Velcro™ fastened near the end of their beak will allow them to carry the food.

Guide children in making replicas of nests using clay, twigs, and dried grass. Dry the clay nests and fill them with play dough eggs of varying colors and sizes. Display their artwork on tree branches firmly planted in buckets filled with sand or plaster of Paris. Encourage the children to do a little bird watching. Provide binoculars and bird books.

1-57029-533-6 *Year 'Round Dramatic Play*

- Do you think that a bird's nest is comfortable?
- I wonder if birds eat while they're sitting on their nests.
- What kind of bird do you think will hatch from our eggs?
- I wonder how the mommy and daddy birds know how to take care of their young?

Literacy Connections

Songs and Fingerplays

Ten Little Twigs

Have children use both of their hands in this fingerplay by clasping them together to make a nest of ten "twigs" for the tired robin.

Five little twigs helped build the nest. *(Extend 5 fingers, palm up.)*
The nest that the robin made.
She built it for her little blue eggs.
So they could have a rest.
Five more twigs helped build the nest. *(Extend the other 5 fingers, palm up.)*
The nest that the robin made.
She built it for her little blue eggs.
So they could have a rest.
Ten little twigs helped build her nest. *(Lace all ten fingers together, palms up, to form a cup shape.)*
The nest that the robin made.
She sat on her eggs for several days.
She was tired and needed a rest!

This Is the Way

(Sing to the tune "This Is the Way We Wash Our Clothes.")

This is the way we build a nest,
Build a nest, build a nest.
This is the way we build a nest,
So early in the springtime.

This is the way we keep the egg warm,
Keep the egg warm, keep the egg warm.
This is the way we keep the egg warm,
So early in the springtime.

This is the way the little egg hatches,
Little egg hatches, little egg hatches.
This is the way the little egg hatches,
So early in the springtime.

This is the way we feed the babies,
Feed the babies, feed the babies.
This is the way we feed the babies,
So early in the springtime.

This is they fly away,
Fly away, fly away.
This is the way they fly away,
So early in the springtime.

An additional poem can be found on the **CD**.

Vocabulary Builders

New Words and Word Study: Help children understand the changing seasons and the warming days of spring. Use words such as *migration, nest, eggs, incubation, peck, hatch, season, year,* and the synonyms of *warm* and *cold.*

Onset/Rime: Words that have the same spelling pattern as the word *nest.*

/est/ *best, nest, pest, rest, vest, chest, west, crest*

Write All About It!

My Egg Class Book

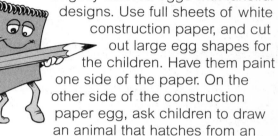

Children will have fun using water colors to paint brightly colored eggs with fanciful designs. Use full sheets of white construction paper, and cut out large egg shapes for the children. Have them paint one side of the paper. On the other side of the construction paper egg, ask children to draw an animal that hatches from an egg. The predictable text will read, *Inside (child's name)'s egg a little _____ grew.* Books like *Chickens Aren't the Only Ones* by Ruth Heller will help children to understand the variety of birds and other animals that hatch from eggs. Bind together in a class book.

Book List

- *My Spring Robin*, by Anne Rockwell
- *Make Way for Ducklings*, by Robert McCloskey
- *A Nest Full of Eggs*, by Priscilla Belz Jenkins
- *Horton Hatches the Egg*, by Dr. Seuss
- *Have You Seen Birds?*, by Joanne F. Oppenheim
- *Rechenka's Eggs*, by Patricia Polacco
- *Baby Bird's First Nest*, by Frank Asch
- *Birds Build Nests*, by Yvonne Winer, Tony Oliver
- *Our Nest*, by Reeve Lindbergh, Jill McElmurry
- *Tanglebird*, by Bernard Lodge
- *The Scarecrow's Hat*, by Ken Brown
- *Not Here*, by Brian Wildsmith
- *An Extraordinary Egg*, by Leo Lionni
- *Chickens Aren't the Only Ones*, by Ruth Heller

Nests, Eggs, and Feathers (The End)

Dramatic Creations: Springtime Birds

Flap your wings and get ready to head north in this seasonal recreation of migrating birds in the spring. Ask all children to participate in this guided drama, and listen to the narrator for directions as they play out migration, hatching baby birds, feeding time, and learning to fly. Children begin this drama by being seated in a circle. Movement is in a clockwise direction.

Narrator: The snow has left the ground and the air is warming up. I see little purple and yellow flowers poking their way up through the ground. It won't be long before the springtime birds are back from their warm winter down south.

I think I hear them now! *(Children begin to chirp, peep, quack, honk, and tweet!)*

Yes, here come the birds. They are flying back to the north again. Spring must be here. *(Children stand in the circle and move in a clockwise direction, flapping their "wings.")*

They're looking for a place to land. They're looking for a place to build a nest. The birds see just the right place. They stop and take a rest. *(Children stop and sit down.)*

Now it's time to hunt for building materials. They look for blades of grass and straw. They look for leaves and twigs. The birds are building their nests. *(Children look all around and pretend to bring back building materials to their position in the circle.)*

The birds are sitting on eggs to keep them warm. The eggs begin to stir. I think the baby birdies are hatching. The mommy and daddy birds will have to find some food. They fly off to bring back some worms for their young. *(Children fly off, bend to the ground to pick up a pretend worm, and return to their place in the circle.)*

The babies are hungry. They eat many worms. Soon they're growing big; big enough to fly on their own. The little birds stretch out their wings. *(Children now pretend to be the babies.)* First, they stretch their right wing. Then, they stretch their left wing. Now, they stretch both wings together. It's time to practice flapping their wings. First, they flap their right wing. Then, they flap their left wing. Now, they're flapping both wings together.

I think they can fly! All of the red birds are flying *(Children wearing red enter the middle of the circle and flap their wings, then return to their position in the circle.)* Now the yellow *(orange, blue, green, purple, white, black, brown)* birds are flying. They can now take care of themselves. When the weather gets cold again, they will fly to the south where it's warm. Then next spring they will return to the north once again.

Published by Totline Publications. Copyright protected.

1-57029-533-6 *Year 'Round Dramatic Play*

Props and Supplies

housekeeping area stocked with play food, dishes, baby dolls, doll beds, dress-up clothing such as business suit jackets and ties, fancy blouses, hats, purses, jewelry, men's and women's work shoes, and work uniforms

Setting the Stage

The end of spring brings two special days in the lives of families, Mother's Day and Father's Day. Round out this season with the opportunity for children to take on these important family roles as they interact with one another in the housekeeping area.

Families come in different sizes and with different members. Roles within families have changed over the past few generations. No two families are alike. By exploring the diversity that is "family," children gain different understandings of and appreciation for what makes up a family. Within the open-ended context of the housekeeping area, have children play the roles they know the best, their family members. Brainstorm with the children what is a family, who are its members, and what are their roles. Write this information down on chart paper. List the commonalities within families such as their love for one another, how the family members take care of one another, and the roles that each family member assumes, and so on.

Many adult family members are employed outside of the home. Provide the props necessary for children to act out this part of their daily lives. Find out which props you will need by asking children what they think their moms and dads do all day. Be prepared to create an office, equipped with telephones, calculators, computer station, and desks. Retail services will require products to sell, play money, and cash registers, and tables for display. Food service jobs will transform part of  the housekeeping area into a restaurant. Professional positions mean that children will enact the roles of teachers, doctors, or dentists.

Back at home, after a long day at work, family members prepare and eat meals, take care of the baby, read the newspaper, walk the dog, and clean the house. Listen carefully to the children's dialogue and provide the necessary support to give the play depth and meaning by means of appropriate props and through your conversation with them. Guide children as they work out the family dynamics. Help them to understand their relationships within the family and with each other as they assign roles to one another and engage in conflict resolution. Family dramatic play is a rich experience for young children and an opportunity for many life lessons. Celebrate moms and dads by providing the means for children to assume those roles themselves!

- How will you decide who will do what jobs in your family?
- Who will take care of the baby while you're at work?
- I wonder how families are alike.
- What is your favorite thing to do with your family?

Literacy Connections

Songs and Fingerplays

We All Work Hard
(Sing to the tune "Sing a Song of Sixpence.")

My mom works in the garden.
My dad mops up the floor.
My brother does the laundry.
My sister paints the door.

Everyone's a helper,
In our house so bright.
We all work hard to keep it clean,
From morning until night.

M-O-M and D-A-D

I've got an M-O-M,
That's my sweet mom,
She helps me every day.
She takes good care of me,
In every W-A-Y, that's way.

I've got a D-A-D,
That's my sweet dad,
He helps me every day.
He takes good care of me,
In every W-A-Y, that's way.

I've Got a Heart That's Full of Love
(Sing to the tune "This Little Light of Mine.")

I've got a heart that's full of love.
I'm going to let it show.
I've got a heart that's full of love.
I'm going to let it show.
I love you, you're my mom, now you know.

Other verses:
    dad
    grandma
    grandpa

Vocabulary Builders

New Words and Word Study: Words and terms in this section will probably be very  familiar to the children, especially the family names such as *mom, dad, grandma, grandpa, aunt, uncle,* and *cousins.* Children may have special names for their extended family members such as *nana* or *papa.* Help children to make connections to those personal family names.

Onset/Rime: Words that have the same spelling pattern as the word *dad.*

/ad/ dad, lad, mad, pad, sad, glad

Write All About It!

In My Family Class Book

To further support the diversity within the family unit today, have children reflect on their own families as they contribute to this class book. The text will identify one family member and one role that they assume. For example, the text might read, *In José's family, his mom works at a restaurant. In Paige's family her dad takes care of the baby.* Illustrate with markers or crayons and then bind the pages together and use this book as a read aloud to the class. The text will invite conversation from the listeners as they relate to the familiar roles of family members.

Book List

- *Just Me and My Mom,* by Mercer Mayer
- *What Moms Can't Do,* by Douglas Wood, Doug Cushman
- *Mom and Me,* by John M. Kaplan
- *Mom Pie,* by Lynne Jonell, Petra Mathers
- *The Kissing Hand,* by Audrey Penn
- *A Pocket Full of Kisses,* by Audrey Penn, Barbara Gibson
- *Is Your Mama a Llama?,* by Deborah Guarino, Steven Kellogg
- *The Daddy Book,* by Todd Parr
- *My Father's Hands,* by Joanne Ryder
- *I Love My Daddy Because—,* by Laurel Porter-Gaylord, Ashley Wolff
- *What Dads Can't Do,* by Douglas Wood
- *I Already Know I Love You,* by Billy Crystal
- *Love You Forever,* by Robert N. Munsch, Sheila McGraw
- *The Relatives Came,* by Cynthia Rylant
- *I Love You the Purplest,* by Barbara M. Joosse, Mary Whyte
- *The Family Book,* by Todd Parr

All in the Family (The End)

Dramatic Creations: Take a Turn

This guided drama will be driven by picture cards in two categories. Brainstorm with children the members of families such as mothers, fathers, sisters, brothers, grandmothers, grandfathers, aunts, uncles, cousins, and so on. Write those family members on individual cards and put them in one pile. Cards for the second pile will reflect the kinds of jobs that family members do such as wash the dishes, go to work, scrub the floor, take out the trash, feed the baby, vacuum, and so on. Write each job on the card in words and accompany that with a simple illustration of the task.

Before this drama begins, allow children to select a family member to act out. There will be several moms and dads, sisters and brothers, and so on. Prepare family member "necklaces" for the children to wear during this drama. The necklace will be a card with the family member's name on it ("mom" or "grandpa") that is tied onto a length of string or yarn and worn like a necklace.

The drama begins when the teacher randomly selects a family member name. The children who are wearing the family member necklace that corresponds to the card drawn will stand up. The teacher randomly selects the task card from the second pile. The children who are standing act out that task. The teacher might say, for example, "The aunt (*Children who are wearing that name stand.*) mows the lawn. (Standing children act out this scene and then sit down again)."

The cards are then put back into the piles and may be randomly drawn again.

Spring Art Activities

Spring Tree: Have children draw the trunk and branches of a spring tree onto a full sheet of light blue construction paper. Use small pieces of torn green construction paper to add leaves. Cut 1" squares of pastel or floral tissue paper. Guide children in using the eraser end of an unsharpened pencil to apply the spring blossoms onto their budding tree by centering the tissue paper square onto the eraser end, by pulling up the sides of the tissue around the pencil, squirting a dot of glue on the end, and then placing it on the paper.

Coffee Filter Blossoms: Create a spring bouquet of flowers made from coffee filters, food coloring, and pipe cleaners. Flatten out coffee filters and lay them on newspaper. Have children use eye droppers to apply diluted food coloring "paint" drop by drop onto the coffee filters. Ask children to observe the colors as they run into each other. Use primary colors to see what happens when blue and yellow mix! Once dry, insert one end of the pipe cleaner through the center of the coffee filter, and then gather the base of the coffee filter together to form a blossom. Secure the base of the coffee filter with tape so that the blossom stays on the pipe cleaner. Add green construction paper leaves secured with tape onto the pipe cleaner.

Butterfly Wings: Eye droppers and tempera paint will create dazzling images on these fold-over prints for butterfly wings. Have children choose a piece of construction paper and fold it in the middle. Open the construction paper and use an eyedropper and tempera paint to drop several colors onto one side of the paper. Fold the paper over and smooth out with hands to evenly distribute the paint. When the children open the paper, they will have symmetrical paintings. When the paint is dry, have the children refold the paper along the existing fold line and using a stencil and trace butterfly wings onto the unpainted side of the construction paper. Make sure that the fold is in the correct place. When the children open their paper, they should have a matched set of attached wings.

Seed Collage: Spring is a time of planting and a time to discover the many shapes and sizes of seeds. Provide a variety of seeds for the children to glue onto tag board in designs of their choice. Dried beans come in a variety of sizes, shapes, and colors.

...lore Spring Fun

BOOK LIST for Spring

- *It's Spring*, by Jimmy Pickering
- *Mud*, by Mary Lyn Ray, Lauren Stringer
- *Spring*, by Ron Hirschi
- *Spring's Sprung*, by Lynn Plourde
- *Cold Little Duck, Duck, Duck*, by Lisa Westberg Peters
- *The Happy Day*, by Ruth Krauss
- *Wake Up, It's Spring!*, by Lisa Campbell Ernst
- *Rabbit's Good News*, by Ruth Lercher Bornstein
- *That's What Happens When It's Spring!*, by Elaine W. Good, Susie Shenk Wenger
- *Are You Spring?*, by Caroline Pitcher, Cliff Wright
- *It's Spring*, by Samantha Berger
- *When Spring Comes*, by Natalia Kinsey-Warnock
- *Signs of Spring*, by Justine Fontes, Rob Hefferan

Flannel Board Props

Create felt pieces for children to use on a flannel board while exploring the following dramatic play themes.

We're Going to the Zoo: zoo animals, "bars" for cages, trees, ponds, and people

Provide five felt moneys for the childrens to recreate the fingerplay "Five Little Monkeys."

The Pet Shop: people, dog grooming brush and leash, birdcage, dog kennel, cat scratching post, and various animals for pets, especially those that correspond with the "Where Is Puppy?" song

The Veterinarian's Office: various animals, veterinarian, stethoscope, examining table, bandages

Butterflies: butterfly eggs on a green leaf, caterpillars of varying sizes, shapes and colors, pupa, butterfly wings in different symmetrical patterns, various fruits, vegetables, and flowers

Children will need five larva and five butterflies for "The Larva's Lunch" and "One Butterfly" from songs and fingerplays.

A Bouquet of Flowers: flowers in various shapes, sizes and colors, stems, leaves, vases, bows and ribbons, soil, seeds, sprouts, a farmer, sun, rain and rain clouds

Many of these felt pieces can be used with the finger plays and songs in this section.

If You Build It…: people, work clothes, tool belt, tools, hard hat, safety glasses, work boots, tape measure

Provide the building materials in "I'm Building a Wall" song, such as measuring tape, piece of wood, a saw, hammer, nails, screwdriver, and a broom. Children will enact "The Three Little Pigs" at the flannel board by using houses made of straw, sticks, and bricks, and the three little pigs themselves!

Nests, Eggs, and Feathers: bird nests in various shapes and sizes, a variety of birds, eggs for the nests, worms, tree branches and leaves

All in the Family: family members representing different ethnicities, clothing, furniture, props to do household chores, such as brooms, mops, vacuums, dishes, food items, and so on